A CHAPTER GUIDE FOR THE LONG SUN & THE SHORT SUN

Michael Andre-Driussi

Sirius Fiction

Copyright © 2022 Michael Andre-Driussi

All rights reserved

No part of this book may be reproduced, or stored in a retrieval system, or transmitted in any form or by any means, electronic, mechanical, photocopying, recording, or otherwise, without express written permission of the publisher.

ISBN-13: 9781947614291 (paperback)
ISBN-13: 9781947614307 (eBook)
ISBN-13: 9781947614314 (hardcover)

Cover image: "Flammarion engraving" (1888) by unknown artist

This work is dedicated to James Wynn and Craig Brewer for their Re-Reading Wolfe podcast, completing three years as of this writing. Congratulations!
I have met James in person several times (Chicago, Seattle, and Chicago again). He is on record declaring that the Long Sun series is his favorite. Here you go, then.

CONTENTS

Title Page
Copyright
Dedication
Introduction
Nightside the Long Sun   1
Appendices for Nightside the Long Sun   15
Lake of the Long Sun   17
Appendix for Lake of the Long Sun   29
Caldé of the Long Sun   31
Appendix for Caldé of the Long Sun   43
Exodus from the Long Sun   45
Appendix for Exodus from the Long Sun   65
Appendices for the Long Sun Series   69
Appendix LSA1: All Timelines (Five)   71
Appendix LSA2: Select Characters of the Long Sun   79
Appendix LSA3: The Long Sun and the Book of Exodus   87
Appendix LSA4: Of the Gods (I)   89
Bibliography for the Long Sun   91
Interlude: "The Night Chough"   93
On Blue's Waters   95
Appendices for On Blue's Waters   117

In Green's Jungles	127
Appendices for In Green's Jungles	147
Return to the Whorl	155
Appendices for Return to the Whorl	177
Appendices for the Short Sun Series	191
Appendix SSA1: All Timelines (Seven)	193
Appendix SSA2: The Divine Twins	215
Appendix SSA3: Of the Gods (II)	216
Appendix SSA4: The Story Orphan Annie Told Gene Wolfe	218
Bibliography for the Short Sun	221
Books By This Author	223

INTRODUCTION

This work is a chapter-by-chapter reading guide to Gene Wolfe's four-volume series *The Book of the Long Sun*, his three-volume series *The Book of the Short Sun*, and the related story "The Night Chough." For the sake of clarity, the seven volumes will be designated with Roman numerals I to VII as a single meta-series.

The Guide is intended to be used by first time readers of each book as well as those who are rereading them. The idea is that we are reading it together, you and I. There are no spoilers, but things will be noted as they are revealed.

Each chapter has a synopsis followed by commentary. The notes cover a wide spectrum of topics, including Technology, Unusual Terms and Phrases, Biblical References, et cetera. After the final chapter of each novel is an appendix of timelines and occasional brief articles; after the final novel of each series is a series appendix with timelines and brief articles.

How to Use the Guide

A reader could read a chapter of the source text first, then check in this book for the notes.
Or
A reader who has already read the entire source text might read this book directly.

Wolf in the OED and Elsewhere

Using the brute force method, here are some applications of "wolf" to watch for, from the *Oxford English Dictionary*:

wolf tree (this is normally a tree that dominates an area)
wolf (slang): sexually aggressive male; homosexual predator
wolf: a kind of fishing net
"a hair of the same wolf" (same as "hair of the dog that bit you")
"a wolf in sheep's clothing"
to throw to the wolves
lone wolf
Wolfland: former name for Ireland
wolfpen: strong box made of logs, used for trapping wolves
wolf-willow

Watch for wolf associations, for example, "crow," a carrion bird that is often paired with the wolf.
Also the French term "Saint-Loup."

Dictionaries Cited
Bouvier's 1856 Law Dictionary (BLD).
Mrs. Byrne's Dictionary.
Oxford English Dictionary (OED).

NIGHTSIDE THE LONG SUN

(Volume I)

Edition cited: Tor (hb), ISBN 978-0-3128-5207-8, 1993, 333 pp.

Dedication: "This book is dedicated to Joe Mayhew for at least a dozen reasons."
 Commentary: Joseph Thomas Mayhew (1942–2000) was a man who worked in the Library of Congress for decades and won a fan artist Hugo in 1998. Wolfe writes movingly about him in the *Locus* article "Joe and Me" (July 2000), calling him "my closest friend."

Chapter 1: The Manteion on Sun Street (9-32)

The priest Patera Silk, in the middle of a ball court game with his student boys, has a vision from a god named the Outsider.
 Silk heads for the animal sellers to obtain a worthy sacrifice, though he has no money. A wealthy man named Blood approaches him and Silk demands money. Blood offers great payment for only a few answers.
 Back at the manteion, robotic Maytera Marble suffers a computational malfunction, during which she recalls the short sun world. A knock at the front door draws her to leave the schoolroom. The visitor is Blood, who wants to inspect the

buildings, because he has already bought the property.

Technology: The text presents a society with a mix of technology levels. The animal sacrifice economy is from the ancient world through Classical times. The ball court technology seems late 20th century. The hover-car "floater" seems futuristic, post-20th century.

Unusual Terms and Phrases

Ayuntamiento—Spanish name for "a congress of persons, the municipal council of a city or town" (*Bouvier's 1856 Law Dictionary,* hereafter BLD).

Bad bit's difference—meaning "makes no difference," from the small coin called "bit," where a "bad bit" is a counterfeit one, worth even less than a genuine one.

Ball court game—somewhat like a cross between basketball and the Aztec ball game played across Mesoamerica, with a little science-fictional *Rollerball* (1975) thrown in.

Card—a large unit of money in Viron, where three cards would be a year's wage for a fortunate common laborer.

Cenoby—where the sibyls, the mayteras, live at the manteion.

Echidna—a major goddess, consort to Pas and mother of the Seven. Grain-bearing.

Fisc—the central bank of Viron, from an unusual English word meaning "a royal or state treasury."

Gibbe—castrate.

Jefe—boss.

Lily—true.

Long Sun—a bar of light stretching from east to west.

Manse—where the augurs, the pateras, live at the manteion.

Manteion—the word for a Vironese temple. See also cenoby, manse, and palaestra.

Palaestra—the schoolhouse part of the manteion.

Pas—sky-ruling god, father of the gods.

Putts—a fool, a simpleton; an objectionable person.

Schola—in Viron, a religious school for augurs, a seminary.

Latin for a place of learning.

Scylla—eldest child of Echidna, she is Patroness of the city Viron.

Subtrahend—the number subtracted from another.

Tartaros—Pas's elder son, god of night and thieves.

Theodidact—a person taught directly by a god.

Viron—the name of the city where the story takes place. The OED lists "viron" as an obsolete word meaning "circuit, compass; a circling course," from Old French.

The (sacred) Writings

Silk alludes to one who beat the sellers, "[T]he Outsider was known to esteem [the animal sellers] last among men already—that according to the Writings he had once (having possessed and enlightened a fortunate man) beaten them severely in person" (I, chap. 1, 17). This combines the episode of Jesus and the Money Changers (Mark 11: 17) with the Gnostic notion that Jesus was a mortal man possessed by a god.

Chapter 2: The Sacrifice (33–56)

At the animal market, Silk is approached by a man selling a catachrest. The catachrest in turn suggests the man show Silk a talking bird instead. Silk buys the bird, a night chough, and takes it back to the manteion, where he hurries to address his students at the end of their day.

After his address, Silk hurries to sacrifice the bird. The bird dies before it can be sacrificed, ruining the ceremony.

Unusual Animals

Catachrest—a little creature like a kitten that can speak, but it always uses the wrong word. One is being sold in the market at Viron.

"Catachrest" appears to be a Wolfe coinage, based upon catachresis, "incorrect use of a word or phrase, especially from any etymological misunderstanding" (*Mrs. Byrne's Dictionary*).

Wolfe makes "catachrest," a person who constantly speaks in catachresis. Punningly, he makes the creature cat-like. (Readers interested in catachresis or pseudo-catachresis are directed to find "Laddle Rat Rotten Hut" (1940) by Howard L. Chace, a version of "Little Red Riding Hood.")

•

Catachrest "words" and (meanings)
"Word, shoe word, who add pan" (Bird, show bird, you bad man)
"Berry add word" (Very bad bird)
"Pack!" (Back!)
"Add word! Add speak!" (Bad bird! Bad beak!)

•

Night Chough—[CHUFF] is another seeming Wolfe coinage, as there is no such bird on Earth. From the description, it is a Red-billed Chough, with glossy black plumage, a long curved red bill, and red legs.

•

High-end Animal Prices
Silk looks over many expensive animals for sacrifice.
Trained donkey—30 cards
Catachrest—5 cards
Fatted ox—3 cards
A sizable flock of lambs—3 cards
Night chough—1 card
Note: David Hendin's *Guide to Biblical Coins* lists some prices from the 1st and 2nd century AD in Roman denarii, which might give some hint as to the value of Wolfe's "bits" (since a denarius is the wage for one day's labor, so 300 denarii is about one year's wages, perhaps the equivalent of 3 cards).
Ox—100 denarii
Calf—20 denarii
Ram—8 denarii
Lamb—4 denarii
Olive oil, one amphora—1 denarius
Bread, one loaf—1/12 denarii

Unusual Terms and Phrases
   Boilin'—stolen object.
   Cant—the slang of thieves and those who imitate them.
   Chrasmologic Writings—the bible of Viron, composed of at least twelve books. The word "chrasmologic" seems to be a Wolfe coinage.
   Cull—a man, a target of a trick.
   Cully—stupid.
   Dimber—skilled, cunning.
   Flash—knowing, wide-awake.
   Hierax—Deathly Hierax, god of the dead, one of the Seven.
   Molpe—a goddess of song, one of the Seven.
   Phaea—Ever-feasting Phaea, one of the Seven.
   Rollin' him over to Hoppy—turning him in to the guards.
   Sacred Window—first mentioned in previous chapter, but here it becomes clear that it is a big television screen where the gods used to appear.
   Sphigx—goddess of the desert, one of the Seven.
   Sprats—children.
   Thelxiepeia—Enchanting Thelxiepeia, one of the Seven.

Chrasmologic Writings
   Silk reads from the holy book, "Are ten birds to be had for a song? You have daubed Oreb the raven, but can you make him sing?" (I, chap. 2, 47). This oracular message to Silk seems to be a blend of Bible verses from the New Testament and the Old Testament.
   "Are ten birds to be had for a song?" draws from Matthew 10, "Are not two sparrows sold for a farthing? and one of them shall not fall on the ground without your Father" (29), and "Fear ye not therefore, ye are of more value than many sparrows" (31).
   "You have daubed Oreb the raven, but can you make him sing?" echoes Job 41, "canst thou draw out leviathan with an hook?" (1); "will he speak soft words unto thee?" (3); "Wilt thou play with him as with a bird?" (5). Wolfe has switched the sea

monster "leviathan" with "Oreb," Hebrew for "raven" (Judges 7:20-25; 8:3; Psalm 83:12; Isaiah 10:26).

Chapter 3: Twilight (57–90)

Silk meets Maytera Marble in the grape arbor. He tells her he was enlightened by the Outsider.

Marble tells him about a thief named Auk, whom she wants Silk to help. After Silk tells her more about his enlightenment, Marble gently tells him how Blood bought the manteion. Silk decides to meet with Auk that evening.

Silk finds Auk at a rough bar and asks Auk to shrive him, because Silk intends to break into Blood's house very soon. Auk shrives him, then has him call Blood's house on the monitor. Silk has a brief, one-sided chat with Musk, who hangs up on him.

Technology: The needler is a standard science fictional weapon. It uses a pulse of electromagnetism to accelerate a small projectile to speeds where it delivers damage similar to that of a pistol bullet.

Unusual Terms and Phrases

Alambrera—Spanish prison, the city prison of Viron.
Candy—easy feat.
Dog's right—a large amount.
Hornbuss—a sexual expletive.
Juzgado—Spanish court of justice.
Nose—turn state's evidence.
Orilla—a rough neighborhood of Viron, Spanish for bank, shore; water's edge.
Prolocutor—the highest priest of Viron, the equivalent of a bishop. "In ecclesiastical law, signifies a president or a chairman of a convocation" (BLD).
Scrape out—religious confession.
Shaggy—general expletive (adjective form).
Shave—con job.
Skylands—mentioned in the previous chapter, but here it is

stated that forests and cities can be seen.

Solve—burgle, rob.

Chapter 4: Nightside (91–115)

Having rented donkeys, Silk and Auk ride uphill to a point above Blood's place. Auk leaves him, taking the mounts, and Silk descends the hill to the back of the compound. Using the rope he brought, he climbs the wall, where he spots a robotic talus patrolling the grounds. When Silk rings the bell at the back gate, the talus answers. Silk tries to bluff his way past, but fails.

He goes around to the front gate, then beyond it to climb the wall. A floater arrives while he is atop the wall. Silk drops down, runs across the lawn, and uses the rope to get onto the mansion's roof.

Unusual Terms and Phrases
Coadjutor—the assistant of a bishop.
Flush his fussock—awaken his wife.
Goldboy—gold coin, here a monetary "card."
Highrider—a type of vehicle at Blood's villa, distinct from floaters. It seems to be something like a hover-cycle.
Jump—energy.
Napped—caught, nabbed.
Pip of the scavy—a fraction of the knowledge required.
Plum—good.
Prothonotary—a type of secretary. "The title given to an officer who officiates as principal clerk of some courts" (BLD).
Sneeze it—to kidnap.
Snoodge—to sleep.
Tall ass—a mocking term for a talus.
Talus—a robotic guardian, like a small tank.

•

Auk Talk, a translation of "cant" (slang of thieves) into standard English, the lines beginning "so I gleaned . . ."

"So I gathered that once he got off work, he would drink a

few beers and sleep like a corpse. Even if I were to accidentally awaken his wife, she would break her broom trying to awaken him, and I would leave the place at my own pace. What I failed to understand is that he wasn't rich, he was in debt to them, so instead of sleeping soundly he was up like a prize fighter."

Chapter 5: The White-Headed One (117–36)

Silk rests a while on the roof. He then tries a few windows and enters an open one. The dark room seems to be the lair of an animal, and he proceeds with caution. The door is locked, and a young woman speaks to him. She is Mucor, Blood's daughter. She controls the lynxes with her mind. Silk goes back out the window and works his way up onto the other wing of the villa. Here he finds a trapdoor, but before he can enter it, he is attacked by a large bird, which knocks him unconscious.

Technology: Talk of little chips of ice that are put into females where they grow into creatures. Mucor birthed the lynxes.

Barsoom: Fifteen-year-old Mucor seems similar to Thuvia, maid of Mars, who has a unique psionic control over banths, the fierce Martian lions.

> "Wait," she whispered, "leave them to me," and pushing me advanced, all defenceless and unarmed, upon the snarling banths.
> When quite close to them she spoke a single Martian word in low but peremptory tones. Like lightning the great beasts wheeled upon her, and I looked to see her torn to pieces before I could reach her side, but instead the creatures slunk to her feet like puppies that expect a merited whipping.
> Again she spoke to them, but in tones so low I could not catch the words, and then she started toward the opposite side of the chamber with the six mighty monsters trailing at heel. One by one she sent them through the secret panel into the room beyond, and when the last had passed from the chamber where we stood in wide-eyed

amazement she turned and smiled at us and then herself passed through, leaving us alone. (Edgar Rice Burroughs, The Gods of Mars, Chapter IV: Thuvia)

Thuvia is a slave of the Holy Therns, the White Martians. During her fifteen years among them, she apparently developed her telepathic powers with banths. The Holy Therns, tired of abusing her and fearful of her power, had recently condemned her to death when she was saved by the hero John Carter.

Chapter 6: New Weapons (137–63)

Silk wakes up alone on the roof. The bird is dead on the grounds below, examined by people who then spot Silk. Silk goes down the trapdoor, through a storeroom, down a corridor, to hide in a bedroom. He gets a needler and an azoth. He meets Hyacinth. She playfully rips up the room with the azoth and Silk escapes through the window. He is captured by guards.

Unusual Terms and Phrases

Azoth—a force-sword, named after the Arabic word for mercury, which in alchemy is applied to the principle of the immaterial.

Balneum—a bathing place, a bathroom.

Beggar's root—an aphrodisiac in Viron.

Lavabo—a basin for washing the hands.

Chapter 7: The Bargain (165–91)

Doctor Crane treats Silk's injuries. Silk is taken to an interview with Blood. Blood offers to sell the manteion to Silk for 26,000 cards, twice the amount he bought it for. Blood proposes that Silk burgle rich houses.

Blood tells Silk to visit a place called Orchid's at one o'clock to perform an exorcism.

By 3:15 a.m. a floater is taking Silk to the manteion.

Back at the villa, Musk visits his bird house.

Unusual Terms and Phrases

Froggies—slang term for the Civil Guard of Viron, so called because they wear green uniforms.

Chapter 8: The Boarder on the Larder (193–214)

Silk requests the driver to pass by Orchid's place. The driver tells Silk what he has heard about the ghostly troubles there. As they stop to look at it, they hear a shout inside and the crash of breaking glass, which causes the driver to speed away despite Silk's protest.

Silk learns that the news of his enlightenment has spread through the city, and people are saying he will bring back the caldé.

Inside the manse, Silk learns the dead bird is alive. Then Maytera Rose alerts him to an emergency in the neighborhood, about a girl named Teasel.

Unusual Terms and Phrases

Caldé—a mayor (from alcalde).
Catamitus—a minor god, cupbearer of the gods.
Ganymedia—a minor god, goddess of spring.

Chapter 9: Oreb and Others (215–41)

Teasel seems to be possessed. She speaks of a terrible old man. She seems to have lost blood. Silk helps out, and Mucor appears to him, briefly possessing Teasel's father. After this, Silk returns to his manse.

Silk dreams.

Doctor Crane visits. He works at healing Silk and the night chough, which is now Silk's pet. At Silk's urging, Crane goes to treat Teasel.

Silk names the bird "Oreb," from a quote in the Chrasmologic Writings.

At the villa, Musk works with a young eagle for an audience

of Blood, Councillor Lemur, Councillor Loris, Commissioner Simuliid, and others. Musk launches the bird on its first flight, and it goes away, disastrously.

Onomastics: In the Bible, "Oreb" (Hebrew "raven") is usually paired with "Zeeb" (Hebrew for "wolf").

Technology: Personal transportation by litter is Classical technology.

Unusual Terms and Phrases
Sellaria—a large room in which guests are entertained.

Chapter 10: The Cat with the Red-Hot Tail (243–70)

Silk and Crane enter Orchid's place. Silk learns from Orchid that the brothel was formerly a manteion. As they are talking, a scream comes from the courtyard. Running there, they find a dead woman with a dagger in her side. The victim is Orpine. Blood arrives and wants it to be ruled a suicide so there will be no investigation.

Silk ponders the case, beginning with the cat image on the dagger. He deduces Orpine was daughter to Orchid. Orchid wants to pay for an extravagant funeral.

Father Brown: Enter G. K. Chesterton's famous detective, Father Brown. A Roman Catholic priest, Father Brown is the protagonist in fifty-three stories, from 1910 to 1936.

Unusual Terms and Phrases
Alambrera—city prison of Viron.
Auscultator—Latin "listener," one of Dr. Crane's medical tools, probably a stethoscope.
A card in a cart—sense of "a sweet deal" or "money in the bank."
Dusted her dial—beat her face.
Flat—penniless.
Ormolu—Orchid's ormolu inkstand. French word for "ground gold," used for an imitation gold made from an alloy of

copper, tin, and zinc.

Rust bucket—a person addicted to rust.

Chapter 11: Summoned (271-93)

Silk interviews Chenille in her room. He tells her he knows she stabbed Orpine. She admits that Orpine was possessed and Chenille stabbed her. Silk advises her and shrives her.

Half of the ex-manteion had been remade into a small theater. Silk begins his work of casting out spirits. He calls out to Mucor, whom he suspects.

Silk has all of the people of the house assemble in the theater. Silk lectures them, watching for Mucor, and when he spots Mucor's features in a woman's face, he casts Mucor out in the name of the Outsider. They go through the exorcism ritual, abruptly halting when an upstairs window shatters and a feminine voice demands that the augur be sent up.

Unusual Terms and Phrases
Abram—mad, insane.
Beat the hoof—ran, departed, made a sharp exit.
Cank chit—crazy child.
Dell—a girl, a wench.
Plucked—drew a knife.

Chapter 12: Dinner on Auk (295-315)

Silk attends a goddess at the window in Orchid's room. After she has spoken for a while, he realizes she is Kypris. She says she was in Hyacinth the night before. She tells him that she is hunted, then she disappears.

Silk returns to the others and they complete the ritual. Musk plays a mean trick on Silk by fake-stabbing him.

At the manteion, Auk invites Silk to dinner at a restaurant.

At the villa, Musk lures his young eagle back.

At the restaurant, Auk and Silk talk. Silk tells of his adventure.

Father Brown: Chesterton's detective has a continuing relationship with a world-class jewel thief named "Flambeau." This begins in the first Father Brown story, "The Blue Cross" (1910), and is further developed through many more. In "The Blue Cross," Flambeau has disguised himself as a priest at a priestly convention, and Father Brown lures him out.

Unusual Terms and Phrases
  Dimber bucks—skilled men.
  Flipper—hand.
  Kypris—a minor goddess.
  Lay—job, as in "that's your lay."
  League—a distance of three miles.

Chapter 13: Silk for Caldé (317–33)

Doctor Crane at his room in the villa prepares a secret report for a place located far away.

At the restaurant, Auk tells Silk about how needlers work, then takes him to meet Xiphias, a master swordsman. Silk's lessons begin immediately.

Afterward, Silk limps back to the manteion. He hears two voices inside, one exactly like his own, and the other oddly familiar.

Unusual Terms and Phrases
  Hacking—sword-fighting.
  Nemesis—the name of an autumnal month in the calendar of Viron.

APPENDICES FOR NIGHTSIDE THE LONG SUN

Appendix L1A1: Timeline for Nightside the Long Sun (two days)

Phaesday (25 Nemesis 332)
12:00 p.m. Silk is enlightened by the Outsider near the end of a ball game (I, Chap. 1).
3:00 p.m. Silk heads toward the market, meets Blood. Silk tells him of being enlightened, and the exchange is witnessed by a group of bystanders. Blood pays him three cards. Silk goes to market. Horn imitates Silk.
Shadelow Silk meets Auk, then goes to infiltrate Blood's villa.

Sphigxday (26 Nemesis 332)
3:15 a.m. Silk rides home in floater; a brick hauler who sees him shouts and kneels.
3:30 a.m. Silk goes to see Teasel, who has been bitten.
Shadeup n.a.
8:00 a.m. Silk sleeps in his manse.
11:30 a.m. Silk is awakened by Doctor Crane and Maytera Marble.
12:00 p.m. Crane and Marble in litter to Teasel's house; young eagle released by Musk.
1:00 p.m. Silk at Orchid's brothel.

1:15 p.m. Orpine murdered.

3:00 p.m. Exorcism and theophany at Orchid's brothel.

Shadelow Silk dines with Auk; they talk about the chalked slogan "Silk for Caldé." At Blood's villa, the eagle returns to Musk; Crane writes note.

7:00 p.m. Silk and Auk go to meet Master Xiphias.

8:00 p.m. Silk returns to his manteion.

•

Appendix L1A2: Chesterton of Nightside

The influence of Chesterton's detective Father Brown shows up in chapter 10 as Patera Silk confronts a mysterious death at the brothel, but Wolfe had planted the seeds earlier when Silk made his strange bargain with Auk in chapter 3, echoing the pairing of Father Brown with jewel thief Flambeau. The relationship between Silk and Auk is a reversal to Chesterton's scenario, however, since Father Brown is mentoring Flambeau's shift away from criminality, whereas Silk is seeking tips from Auk on becoming a criminal.

There is another Chesterton influence at play. The intense pacing of Silk's adventure across a couple of days evokes Chesterton's novel *The Man Who Was Thursday* (1908), which offers a clear case of a man becoming his own opposite, and doing so at a breakneck pace.

LAKE OF THE LONG SUN

(Volume II)

Edition cited: Tor (hb), ISBN 978-0-3128-5494-2, 1994, 352 pp.

Dedication: "For Dan Knight, who will understand more than most."
   Commentary: Dan Knight is the small press owner of United Mythologies Press. Primarily focused on R.A. Lafferty titles, U.M. Press also published a number of Wolfe items, including the collection *Young Wolfe* (1992), the booklet *Gene Wolfe's Orbital Thoughts* (1992), and the autobiographical *Letters Home* (1991).

Chapter 1: They Had Scientists (13–33)

Patera Silk enters his manse to find his student Horn talking with his pet Oreb. Silk tells Horn he suspects Crane listened in on Silk's talking to Chenille.
   Silk asks Horn to imitate him in speech. Silk asks him if he chalked "Silk for caldé," and Horn says he did not, and he doubts it was one of the students.
   Later, Silk dreams of Kypris. When he wakes in the night, he sees Oreb fly out the window and Mucor dissolve into mist.
   Downstairs, Silk questions Oreb, but then he hears Patera Pike's bed creaking. Going upstairs, he sees the ghost of Pike,

which waves and dissolves, leaving behind his calot.

Technology: The distinction between "glasses" and Sacred Windows. "Glasses" are desktop monitors; Sacred Windows are small cinema monitors, each portable by a gang of men.

Unusual Terms and Phrases

Peritime—"a peritime in which the god speaks to you." Meaning something like "a moment outside of time" or "the unmoving axis of time." It seems to be a Wolfe-coinage, using the prefix "peri-" meaning "about or around."

Chapter 2: Lady Kypris (34–54)

Silk is involved in the bustle of preparing for Orpine's funeral.

At the first sacrifice, Silk sees signs of large-scale death approaching: plague, war, or famine. At the sacrifice of doves, a god visits the Sacred Window.

Then she is gone.

Silk tells the others it was Kypris, who gave three messages: one private message for Orchid, one a prophecy that a great crime in the city will succeed that night, and the last a promise she would return to the same Sacred Window soon.

Unusual Terms and Phrases

Mutes—the professional mourners at funerals in Viron.

Skiagraph—the mutes were "the very skiagraph of misery." While this term is used in modern times for a radiograph (e.g., an x-ray photo), previously it was used for an early Greek form of art known as "shadow painting."

Chapter 3: Company (55–77)

For the trip back from the cemetery, Silk rides on the deadcoach. Silk has the driver tell him everything he has heard about the visit of Kypris.

At the manse, Silk cooks up some chops for the sibyls. After Marble takes them away, Silk encounters Chenille and Musk in his manse. There is a scuffle, where Silk knocks Musk down. The message from Blood is that the timeframe for his first payment has been shortened from one month to one week. Musk leaves.

Chenille says she has come to realize she has been accidentally aiding a foreign spy. Silk guesses the spy to be Crane. She says the first information she gave him was about councillors visiting the lake. Chenille suggests that she and Silk get the 26,000 cards from Crane.

Oreb says a man is at the door.

Unusual Terms and Phrases
Dimber hornboys—bosom buddies.
Pluck—draw a weapon.

Chapter 4: The Prochein Ami (78–106)

Silk throws open the door to find a tall augur, Patera Remora.

Oreb gives the dagger to Chenille. Remora expresses skepticism that it is hers, and that she had thrown it, so she throws it with uncanny ability.

Remora says that the plan is to let Musk refurbish the buildings of the manteion and then donate it all back to the Chapter. And an assistant is being sent to help Silk, one Patera Gulo.

Remora leaves. Silk and Chenille talk about how she is possessed by Kypris, without using the name. Chenille stays with the sibyls overnight.

At the villa, Musk tests a large new kite.

During the night, Silk has a nightmare about driving Orpine's deadcoach.

Unusual Terms and Phrases
Hierologics—related to hierology, the religious lore and literature of a people.
Prochein ami—"next friend," a legal term meaning "one who, without being regularly appointed guardian, acts for the

benefit of an infant, married woman, or other person, not sui juris" (BLD).

Chapter 5: The Slave of Sphigx (107–35)

Silk wakes up and starts his day.

Chenille talks with Silk. She tells him about the mechanics of possession, and how Maytera Mint has an accidental fragment of Kypris within her.

Auk joins the meeting and they discuss strategy regarding Crane. Auk warns Silk that Hyacinth must know Crane is a spy.

Silk talks with them about the dwelling places of the five councillors, which turn out to be unknown. And how that hint of meeting them at the lake was richly rewarded by Crane.

Patera Gulo arrives just before they set out.

Chrasmologic Writings

"According to one somewhat doubtful passage in the Writings, the Outsider made men and women of mud" is a garbled allusion to Genesis, the First Book of Moses, where God made Adam from dust, and then made Eve from Adam's rib.

Unusual Terms and Phrases

Anamnesis—reminiscence of the past, especially of a previous existence of the soul.

Brick/stone—"treat him brick and he treats you stone"; deal fairly with him and he'll deal fairly with you.

Dimber cull—skilled fellow.

Dimberdamber—a captain of thieves or vagrants; smart, active, adroit.

Gammon—talk, chatter.

Kink talk—rumor among criminals.

Lodge and dodge—a "frenemy," one whom you help at times and avoid at others.

Plate to me, bait to you—"I'll get the silver plate, you'll get the food"; we both get what we want.

Pure keg—the unadulterated, authentic stuff.
Scavy—common sense, good sense, gumption.
Sharp now—pay attention.
Twig—to espy, or notice.

•

Auk Talk. Sometimes a wordlist is not enough, and a bulk translation is required, as in the case of the paragraph beginning "Only if you go flash . . ."

To set the context of this example, Auk is talking to Silk and Chenille about how to deal with Crane. Auk has said that if they take his money (in order to buy the manteion back), they should set him free, because if they take his money and turn him in, the authorities will find out about the money and they will go to prison, too.

"Only if you play it smart, if you turn Crane over to some nice guys with somebody like me to vouch for you, we'll all be model citizens and heroes too. The police'll grab the glory while we set Crane for execution. That way the police'll give us a phony smile and a politician's handshake, hoping we'll have someone else to turn in another time. I've got to have pals like that to feast one day and flee from the next. So do you two, you just don't know it. You understand I never looted a corpse? You understand I covered it up and left it be? Believe it, I took his money if he'd pay out. And if he wouldn't, why, I turned him in."

Chapter 6: Lake Limna (136–74)

Silk and Chenille ride in a holobit wagon to the lake.

At the villa, Musk has successfully tested his eagle with the kite, and he now sets it to attack a flier soaring high in the sky.

Iolar the flier is hit by the eagle and crashes into the lake.

Silk and Chenille arrive at the village. They split up to search.

At the villa, the kite builder is surprised by Crane, who learns through casual conversation that everyone went to the lake. Crane hurries back into the villa to do some opportunistic searching in the cellars. He discovers the wine cellar. He is captured by Councillor Lemur.

Silk draws out information from an office woman, learning Commissioner Simuliid's activity. He had gone along the Pilgrims' Way to the shrine overlooking the lake.

Silk takes a break with a couple who know the way and urge him not to go in such hot weather. They had encountered Crane. The shrine had been built twenty-five years before.

Silk goes onto the path with a newly bought straw hat. At a vista point he sees the shrine and a man going into it.

Unusual Terms and Phrases

Aedicule—an opening, such as a door or window, framed by columns on either side and a pediment above.

Agardente—an alcoholic beverage in Blood's wine cellar, this is 19th century slang for a powerful drink from Portuguese and Spanish drinks meaning "firewater."

Holobit—one bit.

Chapter 7: The Arms of Scylla (175–98)

Gulo meets with Remora to report on Silk, and the jewelry donated. Remora offers Gulo the prize of being the head of a new Chapter in Palustria. He mentions that the robotic army of Viron, the "arms of Scylla," remain in underground storage.

Gulo shows a letter from a woman to Silk, signed "Hy." After reading it over, Remora calls in his secretary, Incus, and orders him to locate a building where the goddess Thelxiepeia holds up a mirror.

Remora and Gulo discuss the history of the caldé, how the councillors replaced him with themselves. And how the city charter provides for the election of new councillors every three years. Further, how the caldé may appoint his own successor. How the old caldé had a frozen embryo brought to term, perhaps his successor, or a weapon.

Gulo says he suspects it is Chenille.

At the lake, Silk reaches the shrine. Oreb escapes, but Silk is drawn into an underground room. There he is confronted by a talus with a grudge, the talus from Blood's villa. Silk uses the azoth to save his life.

Back in Viron, Gulo has words with Incus.

Unusual Terms and Phrases

Achates—faithful companion, from the name of a character in Virgil's *Aeneid.* Remora, talking to Gulo, uses this word to designate an agent.

Chapter 8: Food for the Gods (199–220)

Silk cannot force his way back to the surface. He goes down the tunnel. After a long time, he finds a flooded tunnel where he lies down to take a nap.

In Limna, a drunken Chenille encounters Auk but does not recall his name. She describes her confusing experience, in that she was at Orpine's funeral but somehow missed it, and then she found herself in a manteion in Limna. So she began drinking until a black bird started talking to her.

Auk has her take him to where she encountered the talking bird.

Silk dreams about Maytera Mint sick in bed, then he meets Mucor. He awakens and Mucor is with him in the tunnel. She tells him to meet her where the bios sleep. He walks down the wet tunnel. He hides when a machine races down the tunnel.

He takes a side tunnel going up. He smells the characteristic smoke from sacrifice. He finds embers in ashes. He is arrested by two robotic soldiers, Hammerstone and Sand. They are under the manteion in Limna.

Unusual Terms and Phrases

Get naked—quit stalling.

Gods—the chem soldiers blasphemously call the scavenging creatures of the tunnels "gods," a wordplay of spelling "dog" backwards.

Up your flue—expletive "Up yours!"

Chapter 9: In Dreams Like Death (221–51)

Auk, Chenille, and Oreb argue about taking the path to the shrine.

Silk sees racks of sleeping soldiers.

Hammerstone figures that Pas "was thinking mostly about the first two hundred years" in his design for cities and their robot soldiers. He also talks about robotic reproduction. He shows Silk a Seal of Pas. Behind it is a room of humans in suspended animation, but there seems to be someone moving in there, so Hammerstone raises the alarm, breaks the seal, and charges in.

Silk follows, and rescues a sleeping woman awakened by Mucor. He casts Mucor out of her, and learns the woman's name is Mamelta. She leads him to a small room that descends for a long time.

Theodidact paraphrase: "The wise learn from the experience of others. Fools . . . could learn only from experiences of their own, while the great mass of men never learn at all." This seems to build on a quote from Otto von Bismarck, "Fools learn from experience. I prefer to learn from the experience of others."

Chapter 10: On the Belly of the Whorl (252–68)

Auk, Chenille, and Oreb are at the shrine, still arguing. Oreb flies off, and Auk starts back, alone. Chenille finds a secret panel and sees a light show.

Incus is working late at the office, frustrated that he will miss a special meeting of his circle of black mechanics. He has been ordered to the lake to find Chenille, to travel there by litter since his boss Remora is too cheap to rent a floater for him.

Silk and Mamelta arrive at a location deeper underground. They find a shaft going down with a spiral staircase. Silk believes it leads to a shrine for Pas and they go down it. She says it is not a shrine but a ship. He goes down a little well into a glass bubble and sees the outside.

Mamelta uses cards to repair a damaged monitor. Silk and Mamelta eat food from the room's storage.

Silk goes into the glass bubble again and sees the terrifying vision of sunrise.

Unusual Terms and Phrases

Black mechanics—bios who are like black sorcerers except they prey upon chems, reprogramming them. They organize into "circles," each like a witches' coven.

Incineratium—seemingly a Wolfe coinage for a basket for paper scraps to be burned; a low tech "memory hole."

Chapter 11: Some Summations (269–92)

On the Pilgrims' Way in the dark, Auk is passed by a possessed Chenille. She dives into the lake. She seems to have many arms. Oreb rejoins Auk. Auk continues hiking, and an hour later, Chenille meets him again. Identifying herself as Scylla, she demands a boat.

At the manteion, Marble suffers in the morning heat. She prepares porridge for Mint. She suffers computational problems. She takes a breakfast bowl upstairs for Rose. Finding Rose has died, Marble starts to take components from her corpse.

Silk comes to consciousness with Councillor Potto looming over him. Silk has been beaten, tortured, interrogated.

Silk wakes up in a cell with Crane. They are in a submarine in the lake. It is the secret capital of Viron. Silk tells how he and Mamelta were arrested when he led them back to the ash heap to get the azoth.

Unusual Terms and Phrases

Subrogative—Dr. Crane refers to Mucor's "subrogative abilities." From *subrogate,* to substitute (one person) for another.

Philip K. Dick: Marble's breakdown within the homey confines of her cenoby recalls a trope often used by Dick in his works. To give one example,

> [H]e saw the dust and ruin of the apartment as it lay spreading out everywhere—he heard the kipple coming, the final disorder of all forms, the absence which would win out.... Reaching out, he touched the wall. His hand broke the surface; gray particles trickled and hurried down ... The chair came apart in his hands ... He saw, on the table, the ceramic cup crack; webs of fine lines grew like the shadows of a vine. (Do Androids Dream of Electric Sheep?, Chapter 18)

Bible: While Silk and Crane are confined together, Silk tells about his enlightenment. He describes a number of scenes the Outsider showed him, including this:

> "There was a naked criminal on a scaffold, and we came back to that when he died, and again when his body was taken down. His mother was watching with a group of his friends, and when someone said he had incited sedition, she said that she didn't think he had ever really been bad, and that she would always love him." (285)

This echoes the crucifixion of Jesus.

Chapter 12: Lemur (293–321)

Silk prays silently. Crane scoffs. Lemur visits and says Silk will be the new Prolocutor. Lemur shows him many wonders and asks if Silk is ready to worship him. Silk declines. Lemur takes both prisoners to attend a dying spy.

Along the way they examine the wings of a downed flier. Lemur cuffs Mamelta into unconsciousness.

The flier is Iolar. He refuses to answer questions. Lemur prepares his execution. Iolar tells Silk that the fliers are losing control of the long sun. Lemur throws Iolar out and he dies.

Lemur takes the three to the room where the councillors reside. Lemur's biological body is there. Crane pronounces the body dead, which causes the robot to go into shock. Crane strikes Lemur's chem body with the azoth blade.

The three race to escape by way of the boat hold and are blown out into the deep water, where a monster eats Mamelta.

Chapter 13: The Caldé Surrenders (322–52)

At the manteion, troopers try to arrest Patera Gulo, thinking he is Silk. The crowd reacts by throwing stones. The troopers retreat inside and Gulo goes out to talk to the crowd. The Sacred Window lights up, and a goddess speaks.

On the lake, Silk and Crane are rescued by a fishing crew. At the village they get new clothes and talk strategy. They have a room on the third floor at an inn. Silk tells Crane he recognized one of the fishermen as Blood's driver. They talk over things and reach an agreement. Crane admits he has a tracking device inside his chest.

At night in the rented bed, Silk dreams.

He and Crane are awakened by guardsmen who recognize Silk as their caldé.

The captain tells that in Viron there was more rioting during the night. One of his troopers says that a goddess spoke to them.

Silk and Crane, under fake arrest, will ride donkeys to Viron.

On the road, once outside of Limna, their group is fired upon by another group with a floater and a buzz gun. Crane dies. Silk performs final rites for him and then he surrenders to the other group, which is thankful they rescued their caldé from arrest.

Unusual Terms and Phrases

Khanum—a female aristocratic title that originated in Central Asia and spread to South Asia and the Middle East.

Quintal—a unit of weight equal to a hundredweight (112 lb), or formerly, 100 lb. Or a unit of weight equal to 100 kg.

APPENDIX FOR LAKE OF THE LONG SUN

Appendix L2A1: Timeline for Lake of the Long Sun (five days)

Sphigxday (26 Nemesis 332)
8:00 p.m. Silk disciplining Horn.
Midnight Silk sees the ghost of Pike

Scylsday (27 Nemesis)
Midday Orpine's funeral and a Kypris theophany.
Shadelow Silk returns from the graveyard. At Blood's villa, Hare and the kite maker loft Flier kite.

Molpsday (28 Nemesis)
Morning Silk wakes up
10:00 a.m.? Silk and Chenille begin trip to Limna by holobit wagon.
10:30 a.m. Iolar the Flier hit by Musk's eagle.
11:00 a.m. Silk and Chenille at Limna. Crane caught spying in Blood's cellar.
11:30 a.m. Mystery "man" reaches shrine.
12:00 p.m. Silk dragged into shrine.
4? 6? p.m. Auk and Chenille at Limna.
Shadelow Auk and Chenille at shrine.
Night Rioting in Viron, where one brigade can barely protect the Palatine.

Late night Auk and Chenille commandeer boat with Incus on board.

Tarsday (29 Nemesis)
Midnight Silk captured and tortured by Potto.
Shadeup Rose dies.
Morning Marble discovers Rose's body.
Late afternoon Silk and Crane escape submarine. Silk and Crane take room at inn.
Night Rioting in Viron.

Hieraxday (30 Nemesis)
3:45 a.m. A captain meets Silk and Crane at their room.
Shadeup Silk's party ambushed on road. Crane dies.

CALDÉ OF THE LONG SUN

(Volume III)

Edition cited: Tor (hb), ISBN 978-0-3128-5583-3, 1994, 381 pp.

Dedication: "For Todd Compton, classicist and rock musician."
   Commentary: Todd Merlin Compton (born 1952) is an American historian in the fields of Mormon history and the Classics. Among his many books are *In Sacred Loneliness: The Plural Wives of Joseph Smith* (2015) and *Who Wrote the Beatle Songs?* (2017). Todd Compton, who became a Wolfe-fan during the *Orbit* anthology years, wrote to Wolfe about *The Shadow of the Torturer* and launched their correspondence. Compton was a graduate student in Classics at that time, so he quickly became a classics resource for Wolfe. They met twice in person, at conventions in San Diego and Chicago.

Chapter 1: The Slaves of Scylla (15–37)

Quetzal and Remora are having tea and sandwiches at the Prolocutor's Palace. Quetzal sends Remora to make him a cup of beef tea, and the moment Remora has left the room, Quetzal repairs his face and extends his fangs. When Remora comes back, they sip and chat. Quetzal tells Remora to write a circular letter to all manteions declaring support for Silk as caldé.

Auk and the possessed Chenille are on the boat on the lake during a storm. They sail into a cave in the cliff. Scylla gives them a mission to stop Kypris, then leaves Chenille.

They argue until a talus comes, the slave Scylla promised. They hop on its back and it tears down a tunnel, into a firefight.

Observation: Quetzal makes an aside to Remora that alerts the reader that Quetzal was the vampire that bit Teasel (back in volume I, chap. 9).

Unusual Terms and Phrases

Ah Lah—"a forgotten god. (Perhaps an alternative name for the Outsider)" (III, character list).

Theonomy—a subject taught at schola, it is ethics according to gods via sacred texts.

Chapter 2: Silk's Back! (38–74)

Marble and Mint must lead morning worship at the manteion without Silk. Marble tells Mint to do the killing and the augury. Mint reaches within herself and finds a new ability in projecting her voice. The sacrifices show signs of trouble in the near future.

Blood and Musk offer victims, and Mint tells him he will receive death soon.

Gulo arrives to announce the return of Silk, and she sees him.

In the tunnel, Incus works at repairing one of the robotic soldiers blasted by the talus. The next moment, Auk wakes up, face down in the tunnel, in the aftermath of another attack. Now Auk has a head-wound and the soldier, Hammerstone, is up. Now Incus is the bully. The talus is dying.

Silk is riding a vehicle along Sun Street and comes to the manteion where Mint sees him. Silk joins the outdoors sacrifice to tell briefly of his recent adventure, and then he goes into the manse to change clothes. Mucor interrupts from the mirror, tells him Blood will kill him on order from Potto.

Observation: The linearity here is tricky, with events leading up to Silk's arrival coming after Silk's arrival earlier in the chapter.

Chrasmologic Writings

"Whatever it is we are . . ." is a passage from Marcus Aurelius, *The Meditations,* II: 2.

Unusual Terms and Phrases

Opticsynapter—this device used by Incus to repair chems is a large, tweezer-like tool for reconnecting fiber optic lines. It seems to be a Wolfe coinage.

Viaggiatory—used by the sibyls for a ceremony held outside, it is an obscure English word (from Italian) meaning "on the move; travelling around" (*Mrs. Byrne's Dictionary*).

Chapter 3: A Tessera for the Tunnel (75–123)

The burning talus gives them the password for the Juzgado's subcellar before it dies. The group moves on. Auk learns a little about his missing time. Incus shrives Chenille. After, she tells of how Kypris-in-Chenille never told Auk about her presence, and how Chenille fears that Auk loves Kypris not Chenille.

Auk, walking along in pain, drifts into feverish thoughts. Ahead he sees the fire of a rocket launch.

Silk is attending to the outdoor sacrifices when the Sacred Window lights up with Echidna. She calls Silk "Prolocutor" and names Mint "the sword of the Eight Great Gods." She gives them orders and disappears.

Silk shouts to explain it to the people when suddenly there is a flash that sets on fire the dying fig tree. Mint gets on a white horse. Silk gives her the azoth.

After she leaves, he returns to sacrificing. Among his many thoughts is the disturbing detail that Echidna had spoken of the "Eight" Great Gods rather than the Nine.

Musk moves to kill Silk, but Marble spoils the shot. Marble, possessed by Echidna, begins to burn Musk alive as a sacrifice to Echidna. She succeeds despite Silk's attempts to stop her. She tells him Pas is dead. Quetzal reveals his presence.

Auk and party are in the tunnels after a fight with people using arrows of bone. They argue their way into another ambush. They win it and talk to their prisoner Urus. Auk teases out that the gang members are cannibals, prisoners escaped from the pits but still trapped in the tunnels.

Auk goes back to find Dace, the old man who had owned the boat. Chenille goes with. They find Gelada, who had killed Dace and started eating him. Auk kills him. Auk's new plan is to free the prisoners to aid in the fight for the city.

French Revolution: The Alambrera as the Bastille, but the Bastille of popular imagination rather than the Bastille of cold historical fact. The Bastille was a symbol of the monarchy's abuse of power because it was a notorious political prison, yet in 1789 the place had only seven inmates. In contrast, the Alambrera sounds like a crowded place of savage brutality, and Auk's plan indicates he will introduce an unexpected column of freed convicts into the civil war near the heart of the city.

Bible: The dying fig tree, apparently ignited by the restarting of the long sun, has ties to a miracle in the New Testament involving Jesus and a fig tree:

> *And on the morrow, when they were come from Bethany, he was hungry: And seeing a fig tree afar off having leaves, he came, if haply he might find any thing thereon: and when he came to it, he found nothing but leaves; for the time of figs was not yet. And Jesus answered and said unto it, No man eat fruit of thee hereafter for ever. And his disciples heard it.* (Mark 11: 12–14)

This enigmatic episode comes immediately before Jesus enters the temple courts and begins driving out the sellers, a famous tableau (alluded to in volume I, chap. 1).

Unusual Terms and Phrases

Bandeau—a strapless top that covers the breasts.

Bufes—the scavenging creatures of the tunnels, blasphemously called "gods" by the chem soldiers. "Bufe" is a term for "dog" in thieves' cant.

Dee-dee—Hammerstone says, "Sand wasn't authorized to give anybody orders in the first place, and I could've told him dee-dee if I'd wanted to." (Oreb says, "Dee-dee?") Possibly military slang from the Vietnam era, where "di-di" (pronounced "dee-dee") is Vietnamese for "scram."

Gipon—tunic.

Jump for religion—enthusiastic for religion.

Thetis—a minor goddess to whom lost travelers pray, here used as a tessera.

Whin—sword.

Winnow—"You want me to winnow you out?" To separate the wheat from the chaff; to clear of refuse material. Here, to free a person.

Chapter 4: The Plan of Pas (124–59)

Back at the tableau of Silk, Quetzal, and Mucor, Mucor leaves the old woman Cassava. Quetzal has Cassava and boy Villus tend each other in the manse. Silk goes into the cenoby, finds a working glass in Rose's room. He asks it about the Alambrera and it shows him live images, wherein he sees Mint directing forces, using the azoth. The monitor tells Silk that Rose had died, which he did not know. The monitor offers to show Silk the last scene it showed to Rose. This is a glimpse of the boat with naked Chenille and Oreb, a scene from earlier in the text (III, chap. 1).

Silk gives Marble a robe. She admits to him that she gave birth to a human boy when she was forty. Silk realizes she is possessed by Rose. This son she speaks of is Blood, who bought the manteion. Then Rose seems to leave Marble. Silk puts Marble in charge of the manteion. Quetzal tells Silk he must become caldé.

The story shifts to Mint, asking three followers for advice. They agree on attacking the relief force.

Back to the manteion, where the pateras set about the burning of Musk and Rose. Quetzal tells Silk the mysteries of the old caldé and his designated heir.

In the tunnels, Auk tries to sleep.

On the streets, Silk and Quetzal talk as they walk. Quetzal tells him Pas was murdered by his own family thirty years before. In some cities, his children have boasted of killing him. Echidna, Scylla, Molpe, and Hierax were in on it.

A horseman rides up and shoots Silk.

Observation: Readers know Quetzal is vampire, but Silk does not.

Myth: Quetzal, upon becoming prolocutor, proscribed human sacrifice in Viron. This detail matches up with the Aztec god Quetzalcoatl, the plumed serpent who told the Aztecs to stop human sacrifice.

Chapter 5: Mail (160–215)

Mint leads the charge attacking the relief force.

Silk, bandaged by his captors, hears news from Patera Shell, who tells about Mint's charge. Shell shrives Silk, then gives him a copy of the circular sent out to all the manteions. In it, the Chapter declares Silk caldé. Silk learns the house he is in is located near the Brick Street manteion, far to the east of his own manteion.

Auk awakens in the bright light of the long sun in his room. After a while he realizes the light is coming from himself (and the reader realizes Auk is still in the tunnels).

Marble goes up onto the roof of the cenoby before shadeup to look at a strange thing in the sky.

Auk is hiking through the tunnels, sometimes accompanied by the ghosts of Bustard and Dace, as well as the mortals Urus, Incus, Hammerstone, Chenille, and Oreb. He has a brief chat with Mint.

Mint has been successful in battle. She discusses plans with Bison and a captain of the guard. She has Bison organize anti-looting units of four. In a captured floater she naps for an instant and speaks with Auk.

Silk meets Colonel Oosik, who has brought Silk's clothes per request. They talk about being on different sides. Oosik hands over the letter from Hyacinth and tells him about Ermine's, a place that has a statue of Thelxiepeia. Silk reads the note and leaves the empty house. After a while, Oreb drops onto his shoulder.

History: The three companies of robotic soldiers and the Second Brigade of the Guard sounds significant, perhaps a historical link. But it does not match the Storming of the Bastille, since the prison was nearly empty (with only seven prisoners), and it was not aided by additional loyalist troops. Then again, it is similar to Viron in that, for a few days prior to the Storming of the Bastille, mobs plundered places looking for food, guns, and supplies.

The stronger historical link is to Joan of Arc at the battle of the bastille de Saint-Loup, an early victory for her (4 MAY 1429).

Chapter 6: The Blind God (216–54)

The tunnel group is arguing about finding Auk after having spent many hours searching for him. Oreb leaves to find Silk. He enters a pit, and then soars up to the sky.

Master Xiphias reflects upon the highs and lows of his day of fighting in the streets. A knock at the door is Silk, who tells him how he made his way that far. Now he must get to Ermine's, on the Palatine held by loyalist forces. He asks Xiphias for a secret route, but then leaves without him or any information.

Auk walks in darkness, hearing ghosts. He hears a woman calling his name twice. The god Tartaros begins talking to him. After discussing things, Auk allows the god to possess him.

Silk uses a strategy approach. Under flag of truce, he crosses lines to bring the pardon of Pas to the dead.

Among the wounded loyalist guardsmen he finds a vampire victim named Mattak. Turns out he became ill after his sergeant killed an augur, Patera Moray. The jeweler tells him this by warning Silk not to come back. In the alley, Silk meets Quetzal praying over the corpse of Moray. Then Quetzal is gone.

Unusual Terms and Phrases

Yataghan—one of Xiphias's weapons, a type of Turkish sword. It has a single-edge blade that curves forward like the Iberian falcata or the Greek kopis.

Chapter 7: Where Thelx Holds Up a Mirror (255–80)

Silk arrives at Ermine's wearing casual clothes rather than augur's robes. He enters and finds his way to the enclosed garden, but before he can find the image of Thelxiepeia, a waiter tells him a tall gentleman requests his presence in the Club. Silk refuses to go to the Club but tells the waiter to invite the man to meet him at the figure. The time is past midnight. Silk sits down, knowing he is too late, as it is Thelxday.

Auk catches up with Chenille, letting go of Tartaros's hand to hug her. She is alone now, the others having chased Urus. It seems that she is the one Auk heard calling his name. Auk relates his experience that basically his dead brother Bustard led him down to the shrine of Tartaros, and now he is going where Tartaros says to go.

Oreb leads Silk to the figure. The mirror the figure holds is only a mirror, not a glass. Sitting down, Silk listens as the Outsider speaks to him. He is awakened by Remora, the tall man. Silk writes a safe passage for him, then Mucor possesses Remora as the councillors torture her to find Silk. Master Xiphias shows up as Silk's bodyguard. Silk plays detective to get Remora to admit how he knew Silk's arranged meeting. But then Hyacinth shows up. After a wonderful reunion, he collapses and is carried away to safety.

Unusual Terms and Phrases

Achates—Remora uses this word to designate an agent. Meaning "faithful companion," from the name of such a character in the *Aeneid.*

Xylograph—a wood carving.

Chapter 8: Peace (281–307)

Marble continues her household chores. That thing in the sky is now directly overhead. It sparks a very old memory in her, of a moment when she was standing outside in a long line on the short sun world. The familiar painting hanging on the wall evokes another sequence of memories. On the roof again she studies the sky thing, and she sees something streaking toward it from below.

Auk shows Chenille the crack leading to the pit. They enter and find Urus, bound Incus, and bound Hammerstone. Auk begins explaining, but then Chenille asks about the airship. There follows a flurry of activity, including an announcement of amnesty for the convicts in the voice of Silk. Hammerstone grabs the launcher from Chenille and fires a missile at the airship. Winged troopers from the airship fire slug guns into the pit. A bomb drops from the airship and a tremendous explosion rocks the pit.

Silk goes through a dream or a vision, then awakens to Quetzal, Xiaphas, Hyacinth, Oosik, and a surgeon trying to get him up. They are at Ermine's, and a big night attack has come.

The plan for peace involves Silk giving a broadcast address and then going around on a floater.

Silk guesses that the night attack was launched by Mint who heard from Mucor that Silk was in trouble there.

Silk gives the broadcast speech, which prompts the Ayuntamiento to offer a fortune to anyone who kills Silk, and lesser fortunes for the murders of Oosik and Quetzal.

Unusual Terms and Phrases

Stade—a measurement of 607 or 622 feet.

Observation: The three threads here (Marble, Auk, Silk) are presented out of chronological order, two of them anchored in time by the image of the missile flying toward the airship while Silk is still heading toward that moment in time.

Chapter 9: Victory (308–34)

Silk and his group board the floater, a military vehicle with a turret. They begin the tour of the city on the way to the Alambrera. When they are at Orchid's place, trouble breaks out. There is an airship above. The floater races and becomes airborne, then tips over so it is upside down.

Auk comes awake after a big blast. There is a hole in the wall, and a floater is slowly falling into the pit. The floater crash-lands. Auk grabs Hyacinth from Silk. A second bomb goes off.

Silk has a death experience. He sees four people, one of them his mother, another the old caldé, the others his biological parents. Silk is sent back to life.

Quetzal has a talk with Silk, reviewing things. Quetzal admits Silk was buried alive. They are all in the tunnels now, the goal being to use the tessera at the Juzgado.

Silk, seeking his cane, unearths a body. It is the surgeon. Silk goes back into the tunnel, digs some more, and finds the cane. Then he is ordered to come out by Sergeant Sand.

Mint, astride her white stallion, tries a stratagem with cables around columns, but things go awry. Her horse goes down and she is caught in hand-to-hand fighting. She frees herself and brings down the pillars with the azoth. Offering herself as a sacrifice to the gods, she is saved at the last second by a trooper named Rook.

Observation: While Silk does not see the missile going to the airship, he has entered that moment and experiences the chaos that follows.

Bible: Silk's victory tour of Viron echoes Jesus entering

Jerusalem in triumph. "And the multitudes that went before, and that followed, cried, saying, Hosanna to the son of David: Blessed is he that cometh in the name of the Lord; Hosanna in the highest" (Matthew 21:9).

In the previous chapter, when Hyacinth hops onto the military floater in her scarlet dress, it looks like a coded callout to the scarlet woman of Revelation:

> *So he carried me away in the spirit into the wilderness: and I saw a woman sit upon a scarlet coloured beast . . . And the woman was arrayed in purple and scarlet colour, and decked with gold and precious stones and pearls . . . And upon her forehead was a name written, MYSTERY, BABYLON THE GREAT, THE MOTHER OF HARLOTS AND ABOMINATIONS OF THE EARTH.* (Revelation 17:3–5)

That the floater in this chapter ends up miraculously flying over the prison wall and falling into the prison pit is drawn from the same Biblical text: "The beast that thou sawest was, and is not; and shall ascend out of the bottomless pit, and go into perdition: and they that dwell on the earth shall wonder" (Revelation 17:8).

In addition to these contrasting currents from the New Testament, Mint's attack on the building evokes Samson and the pillars, a scene in the Old Testament: "And Samson took hold of the two middle pillars upon which the house stood, and on which it was borne up, of the one with his right hand, and of the other with his left. And Samson said, Let me die with the Philistines" (Judges 16:29–30).

Chapter 10: Caldé Silk (335–77)

Marble, Generalissimo Oosik, General Saba from Trivigaunte, and young Horn outside of Blood's villa. Marble carries a white flag of truce and goes in. She talks as Rose to Blood.

The villa contains the councillors and Silk, as well as

Chenille, Xiphias, Incus, and Oreb. After reviewing all the details, Marble requests a private chat with Silk. Blood comes in through the window, followed by Mucor. Blood offers Silk an azoth, but Silk refuses it. The lynx Lion hops in.

Silk reveals that Dr. Crane's death launched the attack from Trivigaunte. He notes that Blood wants to switch sides. Blood makes his offer. They have just worked things out when the others are coming to the door with murder in mind, and Blood finds out that Marble killed Musk.

Blood cuts off Marble's hand; Silk kills Blood with the cane sword; the advancing robots learn Silk is caldé and shoot Councillor Potto.

Unusual Terms and Phrases

Alnico—Marble's face used to have little bits of alnico that let her smile or frown. Alnico is a trade name for an alloy of aluminum, iron, nickel, plus cobalt or copper or titanium, used to make high energy permanent magnets.

Not a dog's right better—"not a whole lot better."

Bible: Silk's two stumbles allude to the stations of the cross. "[Silk] fell as he attempted to mount from the second step to the third, and again halfway up. 'Here,' Sand told him, and returned Xiphias's stick" (345). Granted that his stumbling might be a ploy by Silk to get the sword cane back into his possession, but even so, it echoes the non-scriptural tradition that Jesus fell three times while carrying the cross to Golgotha.

Epilogue (379–81)

Silk waits at a ceremony to welcome a new generalissimo from Trivigaunte.

Unusual Terms and Phrases

Alameda—an elm-lined street. The parade comes along the Alameda.

APPENDIX FOR CALDÉ OF THE LONG SUN

Appendix L3A1: Timeline for Caldé of the Long Sun (three days)

Hieraxday (30 Nemesis)
Morning Storm wind on lake for Auk and Chenille.
10:00 a.m. Quetzal talks to Remora, flies into tree; Remora writes the circular supporting Silk as caldé. Dace's boat sails into cave shrine. Mint starts evolving into General. Silk returns to Sun Street.
11:00 a.m. In the tunnels, Incus repairs Hammerstone; they run into another patrol; Auk presumed dead but revives, sees Bustard. Echidna theophany at Sun Street, she gives orders; long sun goes out, restarts—fig tree burns; Echidna possesses Marble, sacrifices Musk, looks for Auk.
12:00 p.m. Silk shot with needle by Tiger. Battle on Cage Street where Xiphias kills five.
Shadelow Skink leads assault on the Palatine, presumably on Gold Street, which fails.
7:30 p.m. Silk meets Shell. Auk wakes himself up with his own sunlight. Auk talks in dream to Mint. Mint, napping in floater, talks to Auk. Marble goes onto roof, sees airship over lake.

Thelxday

Midnight Silk at Ermine's. Auk with Tartaros finds Chenille.

4:30 a.m. Silk awakens; Oosik has defected to Silk; Hyacinth says they slept for four hours.

5:30 a.m. The airship is over the Alambrera. Silk's floater flies and crashes. Auk takes Hyacinth away.

1:00 p.m. Quetzal and Silk in tunnels; Silk captured by Sand.

Shadelow Mint pulls down the facade of the Corn Exchange on Fisc Street, saved by Rook at the last second.

Phaesday

Shadeup Marble at Blood's. When Blood learns Marble killed Musk, he strikes at her with azoth. Silk, defending Marble, kills Blood.

Epilogue (in the unspecified future)

Shadeup Silk waits at a ceremony to welcome a new generalissimo from Trivigaunte.

EXODUS FROM THE LONG SUN

(Volume IV)

Edition cited: Tor (hb), ISBN 978-0-3128-5585-7, 1996, 384 pp.

Dedication: "For Paul and Vicki Marxen—we go way back."
   Commentary: In his article "The Castle of the Otter," Gene Wolfe writes about a literary event party at his house attended by many notables, including "Paul Marxen, whose paintings hang in my office as well as my study" (*Castle of Days*, 300). A National Arts Program entry for Paul Marxen states, "[He] has been painting for more than 65 years and works in both oils and acrylics. He lives in Oshkoh, WI, with his wife Vicki who is an Aurora chaplain. Paul's paintings show influences from his interest in astronomy, Biblical history and languages, world history and science fiction."

Commentary on Volume Title: Exodus is the second book of Moses. It begins with the Israelites having been slaves in Egypt for over four hundred years. The Jewish hero Moses is born under unusual circumstances, such that he is raised by a foster mother as an Egyptian prince in the house of Pharoah. God calls upon adult Moses (Exodus 3:1–4:17). Moses must lead the Israelites out of their bondage so that they may settle a new land, a land promised to their ancestors.

Chapter 1: Back from Death (15–38)

Mint and Remora visit Blood's ruined villa, trying to contact the Ayuntamiento. It seems that after Silk killed Blood, fighting erupted in the villa, then Oosik and Saba stormed in. Loyalist forces are assumed to have retreated down into the tunnels, but the lack of corpses is a mystery. Remora finds Potto's body, and they learn it is robotic.

Remora's question to Mint is about his secretary Incus, who now claims to be Prolocutor named by the goddess Scylla. Incus offered Remora the job of being his secretary. Remora and Mint argue about this until another Potto enters the room.

Silk is in a litter, talking to Oreb. They race past an enigmatic display in a shop window.

Potto shows Mint and Remora the kitchen. He begins threatening them, first verbally, then with torture using boiling water. Mint bolts but is caught by Spider. The torture begins, but is interrupted when Quetzal arrives to tell of a theophany by the ghost of Pas.

Joan of Arc: Potto's talk of Mint's clothing (26) echoes one of the twelve English legal charges against their prisoner Joan of Arc (that of wearing male clothing).

Alice in Wonderland: Potto's quirky logic with Mint (28) evokes Humpty Dumpty talking with Alice.

Chrasmologic Writings

"O soror neque . . ." Remora uses two phrases in talking to Mint in the kitchen with Potto: "O soror neque enim ignari sumus ante malorum. O passi graviora, dabit Pas his quoque finem." These are slightly altered lines from Virgil's *Aeneid* (lines 198–99), wherein the hero is giving a pep talk to his men. Remora's version translates as, "O sister, we know too well about hard times before this. O you have been through worse, Pas will give an end to this, too." Aside from establishing that

Latin is a language of religion in Viron, this passage also hints that the *Aeneid,* in whole or in part, is contained within the Chrasmologic Writings. (See also "achates" [II, chap. 7].)

Chapter 2: His Name Is Hossaan (39–59)

Silk arrives at Orchid's place and finds Chenille there. Together they talk with Orchid. Orchid admits that Auk has been seen around, but he can't be found now.

Auk talks to his listeners, telling them to get ready to go to a new place, a short sun place. He is a prophet of Tartaros. His god tells him to steal food to eat and cards to repair a lander.

Silk and Chenille ride together in the litter. Chenille asks to be shriven. She tells about possession by Kypris and Scylla. They arrive at the Sun Street manteion.

Spider takes Mint, Quetzal, and Remora down into the tunnels beneath the villa, but Quetzal disappears in the darkness of the stairs.

Silk and Chenille meet Marble, who says Hossaan is there, looking for him. Silk runs to meet him, and Marble invites Chenille to have a meal with her granddaughter.

Silk meets Hossaan, the driver from Blood's, who is another Trivigaunte spy. He says Generalissimo Siyuf is coming to reinforce Silk with thousands of troopers. Marble makes her request about getting her hand reattached. Silk invites her and Mucor to take up residence at the Caldé's Palace.

Silk meets Saba at the Caldé's Palace some time later. They talk about things. Saba is shocked at the ghost face in the mirror.

Bible: At this point, Auk seems to be a Moses figure, since he is telling people to get ready to leave. Also, the detail about Auk having kicked a man to death (I, chap. 3) is parallel to Moses having killed an Egyptian (Exodus 2:12). Going back to Exodus, Moses has a helper in his brother Aaron, who was the first high priest, which fits Silk rather well. So they might be Moses and Aaron, but they each have a bit of Moses to himself.

In the Biblical Book of Exodus there are curious details about jewelry and money, first when the Israelites prepared to leave Egypt, and later on Mount Horeb.

When the time to leave Egypt came,

> [T]he children of Israel did according to the word of Moses; and they borrowed of the Egyptians jewels of silver, and jewels of gold, and raiment: And the Lord gave the people favour in the sight of the Egyptians, so that they lent unto them such things as they required. And they spoiled the Egyptians. (Exodus 12:35–36)

In Wolfe's Exodus, this is translated into the jewelry (II, chap. 5; chap. 7) from the Kypris-blessed heist (II, chap. 2).

Prior to showing the Israelites the Promised Land, God told them to discard their ornaments: "And the children of Israel stripped themselves of their ornaments by the mount Horeb" (Exodus 33:6). Wolfe turns this into the poignant use of money cards as computer chips to repair the landers they were looted from; returning that which was stolen.

Unusual Terms and Phrases
Karbaj—a whip; a scourge; a lash.

Chapter 3: The First Theophany on Thelxday (60–70)

Three days later, Auk encounters Marrow the greengrocer. Auk steals fruit, and Marrow gives him more, and sales go up as Auk is recognized.

Later on, Auk goes to a large gathering at the Orilla. First he goes to a room guarded by Hammerstone, inhabited by Hyacinth. The crowd demands that Auk sacrifice, and Tartaros tells him to do so.

To this end Auk leads the group, including Hammerstone and Hyacinth, to the manteion at Sun Street. Here they meet Incus. Tartaros leaves Auk through the Sacred Window. Auk sets Hyacinth free.

Incus, Auk, and Hammerstone prepare for the first sacrifice, and the Sacred Window lights up with a god. It is Pas.

High above the airship, a group of Fliers soars, led by Sciathan.

Unusual Terms and Phrases
Cank cullys—crazy fools.

Chapter 4: Swords of Sphigx (71–82)

As in the epilogue of Volume III, Silk stands on a platform, waiting for the parade. Quetzal, Oosik, and Saba are also there. The horde arrives and streams by in review. Then Generalissimo Siyuf joins them. Silk invites all to a party at the Caldé's Palace.

Bible: Regarding the enigmatic Quetzal, a reptilian vampire priest, it is noteworthy that Moses and Aaron have a couple of signature scenes involving serpents, first the rod-into-serpent miracle (Exodus 7:10) and second the brazen-serpent miracle (Numbers 21:9). The second one,

> *And Moses made a serpent of brass, and put it upon a pole, and it came to pass, that if a serpent had bitten any man, when he beheld the serpent of brass, he lived.*

might be the enigmatic root of the scene where Quetzal likes to spend time in his tree (III, chap. 1); i.e., Quetzal is a brazen vampire who hangs in the branches of his tree in imitation of the bronze snake held aloft by a pole; and more directly the part where Quetzal cures the boy Villus who had been bitten by Echidna's snakes (III, chap. 4).

Chapter 5: The Man from Mainframe (83–91)

In the sky, Flier Sciathan leads Grian, Sumaire, Mear, and Aer. They descend toward Viron, with the mission of finding Auk. They land among the Trivigaunte. Things go badly. Most of the team is killed, but one escapes. Sciathan is taken prisoner.

Silk and Marble talk dinner plans for twelve, then he offers to take her away to see about her hand. Oreb tells about the Fliers, and Silk has Mucor investigate remotely.

Observation: Mucor's possession of Sciathan made things go badly for the Fliers.

Chapter 6: In Spider's Web (92–118)

In the tunnels, Mint and Remora are prisoners of Spider. Mint naps and has a dream. Talking with Remora about the dream, Mint links Rook to Oreb and supposes that the Outsider sent the dream. Then in another dream she calls to Auk.

Auk is with Incus in the afternoon on the Palatine. They are going to the Prolocutor's Palace. Halted by Linsang, Hammerstone gives them the word from Pas, including a promise that the god is sending help for Auk from Mainframe. And that Pas knew he was going to die forty years before; he began hiding pieces of himself in various bios, and then he died. So the team is searching for Patera Jerboa.

Mint wakes up hearing shots being fired. Spider comes and moves her and Remora from their room to a fresh corpse in the tunnel. Remora tells of how he ended up going to Ermine's after being captured by Erne. Spider tells of his burying customs in this place. Spider tells of Titi (details below). Then they begin to move to another location, but Mint has been putting things together, and she states that the jig is up since Spider's men have all been killed. They find this to be true, yet still mysterious.

Unusual Terms and Phrases

Ken with people—meaning "mingle with, mix with, meet with" in the lines, "I ain't a thief. I talk like I do 'cause we're with them a lot. Spies don't ken with people like you, General, or this other sibyl you call Maytera."

Paid his dial—painted his face (with makeup).

Pay his face—paint his face (with makeup).

Peery a while—meaning "we were watching for a time" in the line "and was peery a while to see what they [the spies had] done and who they talked to."

•

Spider's Tale of Titi: A Translation in Paraphrase

Overview: Spider is telling Mint about Titi, a man who could pass for an attractive woman.

One time Spider and his counter-espionage team were working on a group of spies from Urbs. Things were going well, with Spider's team providing them a mix of real intelligence and fake intel. But one spy figured it out. They could've killed him, but that's drastic.

So Spider planned on getting him pulled. He told Titi to get all dolled up and go around with the spy to three different bars, so they'd be seen and remembered. Then Titi went to the police and said, "I've been raped by this man from Urbs." The police took Titi along to make the arrest.

Spider was delaying the spy with a rigged game of chance.

Titi and the police entered the place, and he cried like two women. The police grabbed the spy.

Mint says, Rape is serious. They'd put him in the pits.

Right, but Titi wasn't going to testify or anything. The whole point was to separate the spy from his team forever by exposure (not to kill him, or put him in prison).

(Then a twist that nearly blew up the whole thing:) The spy ran at Titi, saying, "Petal, what're you doing to me?" Then he grabbed a tumbler and broke it for a cutting weapon.

In response, Titi decked him so hard the spy fell on Spider's empty chair and both fell over.

Titi followed through (this feat of masculine strength) with amazing acting, and the police never figured out that he wasn't a woman. The police showed Spider the door. Titi had to stay to make a statement, and still, the police never guessed. Spider ends with a declaration that he never saw so fine an actor, even on a stage.

Chapter 7: The Brown Mechanics (119–40)

Silk, Oreb, Chenille, Marble, and Mucor visit a shop where taluses are made. They learn a lot about the process. Silk mentions he is thinking about ordering several taluses for the city.

Chenille tells about her time in the tunnels and in the pit when the airship was overhead.

Silk talks about a new design for his taluses, with double armor in front, after learning about the missile that killed a talus in the tunnels. This is in preparation for the tunnel fighting to come. Swallow the factory boss makes the case for bronze.

They look into repairing Marble's hand. The factory can remount it, but someone else must reconnect the optical fibers.

Unusual Terms and Phrases

Brown mechanics—legal robotics experts, who repair chems and manufacture talsuses.

Chapter 8: To Save Your Life (141–63)

Mint, Remora, and Spider enter the room of dead men. Spider says they were killed by robot soldiers, so Mint asks to collect on her bet, since she won. Her first of three questions is how Spider determined Paca had not been killed by Bison's troopers. Spider answers and locks the door. The other two doors lead to a toilet and a storeroom. Noting the possibility of a combatant hiding in either one, he sends Remora to find food in the storeroom. Remora bravely checks the latrine first, then goes into the storeroom.

Mint's second question is about the plans of the Trivigauntis. Spider says they have invaded and are now in charge. Mint's third question is about the original purpose of the tunnels. This leads to discussion on Pas's crafting of the whorl from a large rock. Spider gets into details suggesting that the whorl is breaking down.

As they leave the room, Mucor possesses Remora. Shaken

by the sight, and perhaps realizing more, Spider surrenders his needler to Mint. Then they continue in their task of burying the bodies.

Tension mounts as time goes by. Spider tells Mint that her beloved Bison was one of his, but then he switched over, so he is not the spy in Mint's ranks. Mint draws the needler and tells him to hold his hands up. The robot soldier steps out of the storeroom. Mint has control over the situation.

Unusual Terms and Phrases

Fraus—a tessera used by Spider, the name of a Roman goddess of treachery.

Isagogics—introductory study, especially the study of the literary history of the Bible as a preparation to exegesis (interpretation of the Bible).

Chrasmologic Writings

The first line is said to be, "How mighty are the works of Pas!" Similar to the Bible's "How mighty are the works of God!" (Psalm 107: 21).

Observation: The reader has tension that Quetzal was source of killing, ever since he disappeared on the stairs. This seems to be a red herring. Mint focuses on the only two possibilities she is aware of: Bison's troopers, or robot soldiers. Mint shows her detective skills in this chapter.

Chapter 9: A Piece of Pas (164–83)

Auk's group arrives at the Brick Street manteion where they meet Shell and Jerboa. They prepare for an animal sacrifice to begin the return of a piece of Pas from Jerboa.

Back at the Caldé's Palace, Silk is visited by Oosik, who talks about the parade they had seen. Oosik was struck by the Trivigaunti's lack of machinery, floaters and taluses. This signals that they intend to avoid fighting in the tunnels or in the city, focusing instead on the countryside. Oosik is interrupted by another visitor.

Auk's group continues with their ritual.

At the Palace the visitor is Bison. Oreb and Horn are also there. Oosik departs to allow privacy. Bison admits he has not yet found Mint. Silk adds a place for her at the dinner table.

Jerboa sacrifices the calf. Kypris shows up in the Sacred Window and directs them to the Grand Manteion. She tells them that Pas is currently wiping Echidna "out of core."

Silk welcomes the dinner guests. Siyuf states that Mint was shot, along with Remora. Bison reveals that he and Silk just saw Mint on a glass. Then Mucor possesses Saba to report to Silk that Hyacinth bought the catachrest and is taking it for a sacrifice.

Unusual Terms and Phrases
Gipon—tunic.
Speculation: I sense that Patera Jerboa is based upon Wolfe's friend Joe Mayhew, to whom *Nightside the Long Sun* is dedicated.

Chapter 10: A Life for Pas (184–205)

Mint's group in the tunnels enters a manteion by going up the ash chute. Mint has a tense talk with Urus at gunpoint.

The dinner party continues. Silk announces he will send the volunteer troopers home the next day, allowing them to keep their weapons. This causes debate at the table, where everyone else is against it.

Mint is drawn up the chute. They are in the private chapel beneath the Prolocutor's Palace. Mint cleans herself up and takes a call from Captain Serval, who is reporting that a Trivigaunti unit is mounting guard on the Juzgado which is already guarded by Serval. She then calls the Caldé's Palace to talk to Bison but, pressed for time, settles for Willet.

Silk leaves his own party to intercept Hyacinth. Xiphias goes with him. The others talk about Silk as possibly being a great man, then they notice Quetzal has gone, too.

At the Prolocutor's Palace, Pas has not come for the sacrifices of two bufes. Urus uses the distraction to escape. Remora reads the entrails, which say that he will offer a person. Robot Sand volunteers. Remora shoots him in the face. Pas appears and tells them to carry the robot to the Grand Manteion, where Auk will restore him.

Unusual Terms and Phrases

Killi—a horseback game played by the Trivigauntis, presumably like polo.

Bible: The plan of restoring Sand to life sounds like an echo of Jesus being resurrected after dying on the cross.

Chapter 11: Lovers (206–33)

Hossaan is driving the floater with Silk, Oreb, and Xiphias. Silk spots Hy and they circle around to get her. Hossaan tells Silk about the Trivigauntis at the Juzgado. Then Silk is reunited with Hy. They do some kissing and catch up.

Siyuf and Chenille are at Ermine's. Siyuf is seducing and Chen is pretending. Siyuf brags about the four Fliers they got recently, and another one nine years before. That one showed them the method for wings.

Marble sees a strange procession, including Mint. She has a joyous reunion with her. Mint tells the crowd they are going to meet Auk at the Grand Manteion.

At Blood's ruined villa, Xiphias goes with Hy, leaving Silk to talk with Hossaan. Xiphias comes back alone, Oreb says Hy is crying, so Silk goes to find her.

Abanja is challenged by Vironese sentries. A whisper recommends having a drink at Trotter's. The whisperer is Urus.

Hy is weeping over her loss, and the hard path of her life. Then about how she bought Tick the catachrest and started walking up the hill. Then the lyxes push them to go to the Caldé's Palace.

Abanja meets with Urus, who tells her about Spider and Potto, and offers to take her to Spider and Mint. She gives him a card.

Chen talks to a monitor after Siyuf falls aleep. She asks where Auk is and learns he is now at the Grand Manteion. It is 2:21 a.m. on Phaesday. She calls Orchid and arranges for Violet to substitute for her with Siyuf, since she has to go.

Unusual Terms and Phrases

Brick/stone—deal fairly with him and he'll deal fairly with you.

Cenatiuncula—a small dining room.

Dimberdamber—a captain of thieves; smart, active, adroit.

Know you a dog's right—know you a whole lot.

Lyrichord—a stringed instrument somewhat in the form of an upright harpsichord.

Sauterne—a type of fine wine at Trotter's, the Californian wine sauterne is a white dessert wine, whereas the French Sauternes (capital S and final "s") is an expensive dessert wine.

Bible: Urus seeking out Abanja evokes the action of Judas in seeking to betray Jesus:

> "And Judas Iscariot, one of the twelve, went unto the chief priests, to betray him unto them. And when they heard it, they were glad, and promised to give him money. And he sought how he might conveniently betray him." (Matthew 14:10–11)

Chapter 12: I'm Auk (234–61)

Silk is sleepless in his wedding bed at Ermine's. He has a vision of Horn and Nettle; of Patera Pike sacrificing; of a ragged child weeping; of a blind god; of a small man naked and chained; of a madman among tombs; of Violet embraced by Siyuf; of Auk asleep by the altar.

Auk, hearing his name called, wakes up. All the bios are asleep. Slate says there was no sound.

Sciathan flies in the sky, watching Aer soar away from him.

Auk hears his name called a second time. He speaks to Mint and urges her to sleep now that shadeup has come.

Hy rises from bed in the faint light and works on her makeup in a new way, to copy the face on her wedding ring.

Auk hears his name called a third time. He talks to Jerboa and discovers the augur is dead. Now Auk has the skill to repair Sand.

Sciathan is kicked awake by Abanja. She questions him and punches him. In talking to him, she realizes he must have been possessed by Mucor when things went bad. She has him repeat that he is searching for Auk.

Auk is working on repairing Sand. He says he thinks it was Mint keeping her promise that made it possible. Sand raises his head, looks around. Needler shots ring out, followed by a snarl, and the boom of a slug gun. In the upper reaches of the room, a nephrite image of Tartaros falls with a crash.

Abanja is now being solicitous toward Sciathan. She establishes that he has no experience with horses. She struggles to grasp how the unarmed killer among the Fliers was the smallest one.

Sciathan says that while Aer was alive, he wondered if she loved him as he loved her, but now she is dead, and he knows that she did.

Chen calls Silk and Hy on a glass at breakfast time. She tells about the shooting of Eland by somebody up in the balcony. Slate returned fire and broke a statue. Up there was a dead lynx, Lion, that had been killed by needles. Chen is calling from the Caldé's Palace. Chen then explains her own detective work in finding that Silk and Hy were at Ermine's, through checking at Orchid's, where she found out details about the Fliers and where the one is being held. And that is the bad news, not something personally shameful, but that the Flier is being held in the Juzgado, and Siyuf is moving her headquarters there. Plus, Auk is mixed up with the Fliers, somehow.

Sciathan is sleeping in his cell at the Juzgado when a new prisoner is added. As they talk together over delicious food brought in from outside, Mucor possesses Sciathan to greet Auk. After checking out the Flier's story, and learning that it involves getting Auk to Mainframe by the airship, Auk sets their escape in motion, putting his undershirt out the window and teaching Sciathan how to pick the lock. They escape into a rushing black vehicle before Auk reveals his name.

Unusual Terms and Phrases

Canna—word for propulsion module.

Nephrite—a gem-quality silicate mineral, it is the less prized of the two types of jade. (Focus here on how "silicate" equals "sand.")

Bible: The trope of "three times awakened" proves to be rather complicated in this chapter. That Auk is awakened three times while Mint is trying to keep awake recalls the situation in Gethsemane (Matthew 26: 36–47) where Jesus, knowing that the crisis was coming, stepped away to pray alone for an hour. He returned, "And he cometh unto the disciples, and findeth them asleep, and saith unto Peter, What, could ye not watch with me one hour?" (Matthew 26:40). They repeated this, and on the third time the soldiers came to arrest Jesus. In this way, Auk is Peter to Mint as Jesus. Except that Gethsemane is before the crucifixion.

There is another case, this one from the Old Testament, when God awakens young Samuel three times before giving him information on a fourth time, making him a prophet (1 Samuel 3:3–15). This seems closer to the mark, since Auk is transformed by information so that he can resurrect Sand. Such a shaping makes Auk into Samuel, with Pas as God; except that God woke Samuel four times, and Samuel did not resurrect anybody.

And Auk's act of resurrection of Sand is the primary focus in this scene. As such, maybe the three times is a code for the three days that Jesus lay in the tomb. This angle is interesting, since it puts Auk in the role of the Holy Spirit in resurrecting the Son, as told in 1 Peter 3:18, backed up by Romans 1:4 and Romans 1:8. This seems to be the closest fit.

The falling of the nephrite statue recalls the rending of the veil at the death of Jesus. "Jesus, when he had cried again with a loud voice, yielded up the ghost. And, behold, the veil of the temple was rent in twain from the top to the bottom; and the earth did quake, and the rocks rent" (Matthew 27:50–51).

Chapter 13: Making Peace (262–82)

Silk introduces Sciathan at a meeting between loyalist and rebel leaders. Mint declares that her side has been betrayed. Potto and Loris remain bellicose. Silk outlines the Trivigaunti plan to fight the loyalists in the tunnels, and how this will result in a rebel victory if the rebel arms have not been confiscated. Sciathan describes the airship plan. Silk engages in roleplay as Siyuf, and reveals Chen is the child of the old caldé.

Auk will lead a team of thieves to take the airship.

Silk delves into the mystery of Eland's murder. He theorizes it was a mistake, the intended target being Spider. Presumably by the Trivigauntis.

As a Trivigaunti colonel and a hundred cavalry troopers hurry to break up the meeting, Loris makes his statement. Silk surrenders. Trivigaunti spy forces led by Hossaan enter the room. Shooting erupts.

Chrasmologic Writings

The Writings mention a rain of blood, plagues, and famines. This reminds one of the Ten Plagues of Egypt, from water into blood to the death of the firstborn. But rain of blood is different from water into blood. Blood rain is found in Homer's *Iliad* and subsequent works.

Observation: The narrator's dramatic and late unmasking as the student Horn, "At that moment I burst into the room." Another surprise is that Chenille is a natural child of Caldé Tussah, a notion first floated by Patera Gulo (II, chap. 5) at a point where it seemed obviously ridiculous.

Chapter 14: The Best Thieves in the Whorl (283–320)

In a tent at night, Horn and Nettle talk with Silk. It turns out Loris is now dead, killed after he shot the spies. Marble joins the talk. Silk talks about the dead woman in the tunnels below the shrine. Nettle asks about Silk's surrender, and he explains it. Oreb joins the party. Remora asks who killed Eland, and Silk says he thinks it was Hossaan.

Outside at midday, Silk and others stand as the airship moves above. They are going to be taken to the Rani in Trivigaunte.

Sand and Hammerstone storm into Ermine's to talk with Siyuf.

Scleroderma, looking for Moly (Marble) at the Caldé's Palace, finds Xiphias, who takes her to Mucor.

Oreb flies over the airship, then dives to attack.

A Trivigaunti pterotrooper has a new pet, a catachrest. Suddenly they are attacked by a black bird.

Siyuf meets Sand and Hammerstone, who want Moly (Marble) and Incus from the prisoners. There are eighty-two prisoners. The robots say that the Vironese have united against the Trivigauntis, so returning Silk is the only hope. The bad news is that the airship left an hour before. So the robots take Siyuf and Violet hostage.

On the airship, Silk's group struggles to get their "sea legs" in the air. The thieves talk over their plan. Silk decides he must act first to save them all. Abruptly he climbs out the window and up onto the roof of the gondola. Mucor shows up there in ghostly form, and they talk. Silk climbs up one of the cables connecting the gondola to the balloon structure.

Tick the catachrest comes in through a window. Auk brings him to Hy. Then Oreb and Silk enter.

Hadale confronts Silk, who had been missing an hour ago. They negotiate to talk in the cockpit.

Back at Viron, Mint's group meets with their prisoner

Siyuf. Mint states that Trivigaunte declared war on Viron an hour before. Councillors Potto and Newt are also there. Mint says Viron is reunited. They want to trade Siyuf for Silk, but the Trivigauntis won't even talk about it. Some believe there is internal politics going on, but Potto claims the airship is wrecked or off course. Then they reveal their ploy, a robot copy of Siyuf, that they will release.

On the airship, three of the engines have quit. Saba is under guard after having been possessed by Mucor. A fourth engine dies. Major Hadale aims to land in the desert by a caravan.

Unusual Terms and Phrases

'ishsh—an (airship) elevator, from an Arabic word meaning "to nest."

Observation: The "sea legs" on the airship is a strange deal.

Philip K. Dick: The robotic copy of Siyuf seems like another nod to Philip K. Dick, who was famously fond of the trope. At first glance, it seems unusually quick and easy that Mint's group has whipped up a robot copy within a few days, when manufacturing a talus seems to take longer. Then again, the task is not building a chem, it is reshaping a chem, which is the realm of the black mechanics. Patera Incus is, of course, a black mechanic, but he is hardly alone: Bittersweet, Fulmar, and Patera Tussah are members; perhaps Patera Shell and/or Maytera Maple are members as well.

Chapter 15: To Mainframe! (321–46)

Auk's group is maneuvering to seize control of the grounded airship. A shot is fired.

Silk and Hyacinth are in the cockpit when they hear the shot fired. Hyacinth overpowers the pilot.

Silk goes out for some quiet time and nearly jumps off the gondola. Horn finds him and they talk. Horn tells of his intent to write a book about Silk. Then Mucor possesses Horn and he starts to slide off.

Auk visits the cockpit, looking for Silk. Silk arrives and announces they will now return the airship command to Saba. They go to use the glass to call Trivigaunte and Kypris comes on with a message for Silk, an offer for him to be scanned and merge with Pas.

Observation: Silk exhibits near-suicidal behavior.

Bible: This "merge with Pas" notion seems like the heresy of a trinity made up of Jehovah, his wife, and their son. Compounding this is the strong possibility that Silk's biological blond parents, whom he saw in his near-death experience (III, chap. 9), were in fact the mortals behind "Pas" and "Kypris."

Chapter 16: Exodus from the Long Sun (347–70)

Silk's group sees Auk's lander shrink away. Back at the airship, they begin their return flight.

In Viron, it is snowing. There has been fighting in the Sun Street Quarter. Mint is moving among the refugees. She encounters Marble, who now goes by Magnesia, and says she is about to become an abandoned woman. Mint meets Mucor for the first time, and Mucor is waking up sleepers in their glass coffins.

The airship is back, giving air support; Quetzal was around, talking to the refugees about leaving the whorl, then Silk took him away, so Mint learns that Silk is back.

Bison is about to lead an assault. As Mint rushes to meet him at the old boathouse, she sees Silk and Hyacinth on a white horse.

Silk and Hyacinth arrive at the crater-exposed portal to the tunnels. They have taken all the cards from the Fisc to repair the landers. Turns out the robot Siyuf is leading the Trivigauntis in battle.

Hyacinth goes into the tunnel. Horn stops Silk from following her. Silk asks if it is all about the tryst that Hyacinth had with Saba on the airship. Horn says no, but he gives Silk a needler to kill her with. Silk talks Hyacinth's rationale with

Horn, and then her history. Then they move to enter the tunnel, but Hyacinth refuses to leave the whorl. She runs off and Silk follows, ordering Horn and Nettle into the tunnel. He vows to bring her to meet them at their lander or via another lander.

Bible: In the Book of Exodus, God told the Israelites to sacrifice their ornaments at Horeb, the exact location where God had spoken to Moses through the burning bush: "And the children of Israel stripped themselves of their ornaments by the mount Horeb" (Exodus 33:6). Wolfe turns this into the use of money cards as computer chips to repair the lander they were looted from; and to do this action at the precise location where Silk first saw the true sun of the outside.

When Silk tells Horn at the tunnel about Hyacinth, he seems to be showing through his actions the New Testament's statement on Love:

> *Love is patient and kind. Love is not jealous or boastful or proud or rude. It does not demand its own way. It is not irritable, and it keeps no record of being wronged. It does not rejoice about injustice but rejoices whenever the truth wins out. Love never gives up, never loses faith, is always hopeful, and endures through every circumstance.* (1 Corinthians 13:4–7 NLT)

Thus, Silk will not kill Hyacinth out of jealousy, which is the most immediate thing, an action that Horn expects. At the reflecting pool in Ermine's, the Outsider told Silk that Kypris is moving toward the Outsider, since the Outsider is the source of love (III, chap. 7). But this promise of victory in the long term is complicated by the messy fact that the goddess of love is more accurately a goddess of lust, and we are left at the human scale with the vision of a semi-Jesus refusing to give up on a semi-scarlet woman in the city of destruction.

My Defense (371–82)

Horn tells about the making of this work on the planet Blue. He gives notes on Marble, Auk, Hyacinth, and Mint. Less on Blood, Musk, Crane, and Incus. He identifies Quetzal as an "inhumu."

This segues into their path in the tunnel to the lander, a time when Horn and Nettle walked alone for a while with Quetzal. Then later, at the camp, Mucor tells Horn that Marble is weeping, carrying Quetzal. He was shot by Triv soldiers.

The refugees had to fight Trivs on their way to the lander area, where they and the sleepers filled two landers. Quetzal died, and they went to Blue.

Horn has not seen Silk since. He lives on an island with his wife Nettle and their sons.

Bible: In the Bible's Exodus, Moses leads the Israelites out of their captivity in Egypt and to the Promised Land, but he does not himself enter the Promised Land. As revealed in Deuteronomy, the Fifth Book of Moses:

> *And the Lord said unto him, This is the land which I sware unto Abraham, unto Isaac, and unto Jacob, saying, I will give it unto thy seed: I have caused thee to see it with thine eyes, but thou shalt not go over thither. So Moses the servant of the Lord died there in the land of Moab, according to the word of the Lord.* (Deuteronomy 34:4–5)

Wolfe's Silk does not go to Blue because of Hyacinth. Wolfe's Quetzal does not go to Blue because he dies on the lander. Wolfe's Auk does not go to Blue because he goes to Green.

Afterward (383–84)

Horn finishes writing, asks the twins where their brother Sinew is. Planet Green is near, raising storms and tides. Horn sees the Whorl in the sky, and an ominous flying thing.

APPENDIX FOR EXODUS FROM THE LONG SUN

Appendix L4A1: Timeline for Exodus From the Long Sun (ten days)

Sphigxday
Shadelow Mint talks to Sand about strategy of sending chem soldiers into the tunnels (chap. 8)

Scylsday
Day Silk sends Guardsman to Orchid's looking for Auk, Hy, Chenille, but they return empty-handed (chap. 2). Marble visits Marl, learns about Swallow's shop of brown mechanics (chap. 2).

Molpsday
Shadeup Quetzal witnesses Pas theophany at Grand Manteion (chap. 1). Mint and Remora captured by Potto at ruins of Blood's villa (chap. 1).
Midday Silk meets Chenille, Orchid at Orchid's (chap. 2). Auk the Prophet preaching. Silk meets Hossaan who says Siyuf and troopers will arrive in three or four days (chap. 2). Silk meets Saba who glimpses Mucor in mirror.

Tarsday

Hieraxday

Thelxday
Midday Tartaros leaves Auk (chap. 3). Tartaros tells Fliers to find Auk (chap. 13). Auk releases Hy (chap. 3). Pas theophany at Sun Street for Auk, Incus, Hammerstone (chap. 3). Trivigaunti parade (chap. 4). Fliers land (chap. 5).
Shadelow Auk, Incus, Hammerstone at Brick Street (chap. 9). Kypris theophany at Brick Street, tells them to take Jerboa to the Grand Manteion (chap. 9).
7:30 p.m. Mint and Remora rescued in the tunnels (chap. 8).
8:00 p.m. Dinner with Caldé (chap. 9). Mint, Spider, Remora, Urus, Sand, Schist, Eland, and Slate at Prolocutor's Palace (chap. 10). Sand sacrificed to Pas theophany in Prolocutor's Palace, tells them to take Sand to the Grand Manteion (chap. 10).
8:30 p.m. Silk spots Hyacinth on Gold Street, and their reunion (chap. 11). Chenille at Ermine's with Siyuf (chap. 11). Abanja at Trotter's with Urus (chap. 11).

Phaesday
2:21 a.m. Chenille calls Orchid (chap. 11). Marriages: Silk and Hyacinth; Hammerstone and Moly (Marble/Rose). Silk has second enlightenment. Auk awakened first time (chap. 12).
Shadeup Auk awakened second time, tells Mint to sleep (chap. 12)
7:00 a.m.? Auk awakened third time, by voice from the Sacred Window (chap. 12); repairs Sand.
8:00 a.m.? Chenille calls Silk and Hy at Ermine's (chap. 12). Trivigauntis take control of the Juzgado. Mucor possesses Sciathan again. Auk helps Sciathan escape Juzgado (chap. 12)

Sphigxday
Night Meeting between Insurgents and Ayuntamiento; Silk

surrenders Viron to Potto; Hossaan takes the Insurgents prisoner (chap. 13).

Scylsday
Shadeup Viron forms new government, declaring Silk caldé.
7:00 a.m. Prisoners put onto airship (chap. 14).
8:00 a.m. Hammerstone and Sand at Ermine's take Siyuf and Violet hostage to exchange for Silk and Marble (chap. 14). Mucor possesses Saba, orders airship to head east (chap. 14). It goes east for an hour (chap. 14).
3:00 p.m. Second Siyuf (chem) revealed (chap. 14).
4:00 p.m. Silk and Horn on gondola roof (chap. 15). Kypris's temptation of Silk (chap. 15).
Shadelow Airship, pushed along by strong wind, arrives at Mainframe.

Molpsday
Shadeup Auk, Chenille, Gib (and others) leave Whorl on first lander (chap. 16). Departure from Mainframe (chap. 16). Hy and Saba have sex while Horn distracts Silk (chap. 16).
3:00 p.m. Airship arrives back at Viron, where winter has hit and renewed fighting has broken out. Mint in Orilla (chap. 16). Bison about to attack (chap. 16). Silk and Hyacinth on horseback (chap. 16). The Vironese exodus begins with the people of the Sun Street quarter going into the tunnels.

APPENDICES FOR THE LONG SUN SERIES

APPENDIX LSA1: ALL TIMELINES (FIVE)

0. History of the Long Sun

Years Ago: Event

332: Magnesia waits to board Whorl. Whorl launched. 1000 years ago objective time (III, chap. 6).

200: Caddis witnesses theophanies of Echidna, Tartaros, Scylla, and Pas (I, chap. 6).

184: Marble last entered attic (III, chap. 5).

100: Hydromancy discontinued (II, chap. 6). End of Pas's planned time (II, chap. 9).

81: Jerboa born (III, chap. 5).

61: Jerboa arrives at Brick Street manteion (IV, chap. 9).

60: Rose arrives at Sun Street manteion.

56: Crane born (II, chap. 13).

52: Marble begins teaching (I, chap. 3).

50?: Rose loses first arm to disease (III, chap. 10).

50: Scylla last appeared in a Sacred Window.

46: Rose loses track of Blood's foster mother (III, chap. 10).

45: Orchid born.

43: Swallow born (IV, chap. 7). Rose becomes senior sibyl at Sun Street manteion (III, chap. 4).

40: Prosimians become councillors (II, chap. 6). Pas hides fragments of himself (IV, chap. 6).

33: Quetzal becomes head of Chapter (III, character list).

30: Pas wiped out of core. Xiphias loses leg to treachery (I, chap. 13).
25: Loris builds Scylla shrine (II, chap. 6). Lemur first thinks of flight (II, chap. 12).
23: Silk born, Hyacinth born.
22: Tussah dies, according to Crane (II, chap. 12). Spider expelled from the Guard, starts working for Potto (IV, chap. 6).
21: Talus-to-fail built (IV, chap. 7).
20: Tussah dies (allowing for Chenille to be conceived while he is alive). The penultimate time Blood spoke to his foster mother (III, chap. 10). Trivigauntis allow men to use scissors (IV, chap. 4).
19: Chenille born (lists).
18: Orchid's monitor out of service (IV, chap. 11). Orpine born (Case #1). Siyuf joins regiment (IV, chap. 4).
16: Swallow paid for a talus failure (IV, chap. 7).
15: Mucor born (lists).
14: Orpine born, if Mucor was Orchid's first (Case #2).
11: Silk (12 years old) breaks into abandoned house, requires glasses to read.
10: Brain surgeon works on Mucor (II, chap. 11). Silk enters schola.
9: Hyacinth seduced by commissioner. Trivigauntis kill a Flier, get pattern for wings (IV, chap. 11).
5: Orpine (age 13) comes to Orchid's (if Case #1).
4: Crane begins working for Blood (I, chap. 7). Hy leaves Orchid's for Blood's villa. Silk's mother dies.
2: Silk graduates (III, chap. 7). Silk arrives at Sun Street manteion.
1: Orpine (age 13) comes to Orchid's (if Case #2). Pike shrives Auk (I, chap. 3), dies in Spring (II, chap. 1). Most recent burial in Spider's graveyard, last Spring (Titi?) (IV, chap. 8).
.25: Orchid's place is haunted.
.16: Simuliid goes to Lake Shrine (II, chap. 6).
.16: Crane goes to Lake Shrine (II, chap. 6).

❖ ❖ ❖

1. Timeline for Nightside the Long Sun (two days)

Phaesday (25 Nemesis 332)
12:00 p.m. Silk is enlightened by the Outsider near the end of a ball game (I, Chap. 1).
3:00 p.m. Silk heads toward the market, meets Blood. Silk tells him of being enlightened, and the exchange is witnessed by a group of bystanders. Blood pays him three cards. Silk goes to market. Horn imitates Silk.
Shadelow Silk meets Auk, then goes to infiltrate Blood's villa.

Sphigxday (26 Nemesis 332)
3:15 a.m. Silk rides home in floater; a brick hauler who sees him shouts and kneels.
3:30 a.m. Silk goes to see Teasel, who has been bitten.
Shadeup n.a.
8:00 a.m. Silk sleeps in his manse.
11:30 a.m. Silk is awakened by Doctor Crane and Maytera Marble.
12:00 p.m. Crane and Marble in litter to Teasel's house; young eagle released by Musk.
1:00 p.m. Silk at Orchid's brothel.
1:15 p.m. Orpine murdered.
3:00 p.m. Exorcism and theophany at Orchid's brothel.
Shadelow Silk dines with Auk; they talk about the chalked slogan "Silk for Caldé." At Blood's villa, the eagle returns to Musk; Crane writes note.
7:00 p.m. Silk and Auk go to meet Master Xiphias.
8:00 p.m. Silk returns to his manteion.

2. Timeline for Lake of the Long Sun (five days)

Sphigxday (26 Nemesis 332)
8:00 p.m. Silk disciplining Horn.
Midnight Silk sees the ghost of Pike.

Scylsday (27 Nemesis)
Midday Orpine's funeral and a Kypris theophany.
Shadelow Silk returns from the graveyard. At Blood's villa, Hare and the kite maker loft Flier kite.

Molpsday (28 Nemesis)
Morning Silk wakes up
10:00 a.m.? Silk and Chenille begin trip to Limna by wagon.
10:30 a.m. Iolar the Flier hit by Musk's eagle.
11:00 a.m. Silk and Chenille at Limna. Crane caught spying in Blood's cellar.
11:30 a.m. Mystery "man" reaches shrine.
12:00 p.m. Silk dragged into shrine.
4? 6? p.m. Auk and Chenille at Limna.
Shadelow Auk and Chenille at shrine.
Night Rioting in Viron, where one brigade can barely protect the Palatine.
Late night Auk and Chenille commandeer boat with Incus on board.

Tarsday (29 Nemesis)
Midnight Silk captured and tortured by Potto.
Shadeup Rose dies.
Morning Marble discovers Rose's body.
Late afternoon Silk and Crane escape submarine. Silk and Crane take room at inn.
Night Rioting in Viron.

Hieraxday (30 Nemesis)
3:45 a.m. A captain meets Silk and Crane at their room. Shadeup Silk's party ambushed on road. Crane dies.

3. Timeline for Caldé of the Long Sun (three days)

Hieraxday (30 Nemesis)
Morning Storm wind on lake for Auk and Chenille.
10:00 a.m. Quetzal talks to Remora, flies into tree; Remora writes the circular supporting Silk for Caldé. Dace's boat sails into cave shrine. Mint starts evolving into General. Silk returns to Sun Street.
11:00 a.m. In the tunnels, Incus repairs Hammerstone; they run into another patrol; Auk presumed dead but revives, sees Bustard. Echidna theophany at Sun Street, she gives orders; long sun goes out, restarts—fig tree burns; Echidna possesses Marble, sacrifices Musk, looks for Auk.
12:00 p.m. Silk shot with needle by Tiger. Battle on Cage Street where Xiphias kills five.
Shadelow Skink leads assault on the Palatine, presumably on Gold Street, which fails.
7:30 p.m. Silk meets Shell. Auk wakes himself up with his own sunlight. Auk talks in dream to Mint. Mint, napping in floater, talks to Auk. Marble goes onto roof, sees airship over lake.

Thelxday
Midnight Silk at Ermine's. Auk with Tartaros finds Chenille.
4:30 a.m. Silk awakens; Oosik has defected to Silk; Hyacinth says they slept for four hours.
5:30 a.m. The airship is over the Alambrera. Silk's floater flies and crashes. Auk takes Hyacinth away.
1:00 p.m. Quetzal and Silk in tunnels; Silk captured by Sand.

Shadelow Mint pulls down the fascade of the Corn Exchange on Fisc Street, saved by Rook at the last second.

Phaesday
Shadeup Marble at Blood's. When Blood learns Marble killed Musk, he strikes at her with azoth. Silk, defending Marble, kills Blood.

Epilogue (in the unspecified future)
Shadeup Silk waits at a ceremony to welcome a new generalissimo from Trivigaunte.

4. Timeline for Exodus From the Long Sun (ten days)

Sphigxday
Shadelow Mint talks to Sand about strategy of sending chem soldiers into the tunnels (chap. 8).

Scylsday
Day Silk sends Guardsman to Orchid's looking for Auk, Hy, Chenille, but they return empty-handed (chap. 2). Marble visits Marl, learns about Swallow's shop of brown mechanics (chap. 2).

Molpsday
Shadeup Quetzal witnesses Pas theophany at Grand Manteion (chap. 1). Mint and Remora captured by Potto at ruins of Blood's villa (chap. 1).
Midday Silk meets Chenille, Orchid at Orchid's (chap. 2). Auk the Prophet preaching. Silk meets Hossaan who says Siyuf and troopers will arrive in three or four days (chap. 2). Silk meets Saba who glimpses Mucor in mirror.

Tarsday

Hieraxday

Thelxday

Midday Tartaros leaves Auk (chap. 3). Tartaros tells Fliers to find Auk (chap. 13). Auk releases Hy (chap. 3). Pas theophany at Sun Street for Auk, Incus, Hammerstone (chap. 3). Trivigaunti parade (chap. 4). Fliers land (chap. 5).

Shadelow Auk, Incus, Hammerstone at Brick Street (chap. 9). Kypris theophany at Brick Street, tells them to take Jerboa to the Grand Manteion (chap. 9).

7:30 p.m. Mint and Remora rescued in the tunnels (chap. 8).

8:00 p.m. Dinner with Caldé (chap. 9). Mint, Spider, Remora, Urus, Sand, Schist, Eland, and Slate at Prolocutor's Palace (chap. 10). Sand sacrificed to Pas theophany in Prolocutor's Palace, tells them to take Sand to the Grand Manteion (chap. 10).

8:30 p.m. Silk spots Hyacinth on Gold Street, and their reunion (chap. 11). Chenille at Ermine's with Siyuf (chap. 11). Abanja at Trotter's with Urus (chap. 11).

Phaesday

2:21 a.m. Chenille calls Orchid (chap. 11). Marriages: Silk and Hyacinth; Hammerstone and Moly (Marble/Rose). Silk has second enlightenment. Auk awakened first time (chap. 12).

Shadeup Auk awakened second time, tells Mint to sleep (chap. 12).

7:00 a.m.? Auk awakened third time, by voice from the Sacred Window (chap. 12); repairs Sand.

8:00 a.m.? Chenille calls Silk and Hy at Ermine's (chap. 12). Trivigauntis take control of the Juzgado. Mucor possesses Sciathan again. Auk helps Sciathan escape Juzgado (chap. 12).

Sphigxday

Night Meeting between Insurgents and Ayuntamiento; Silk

surrenders Viron to Potto; Hossaan takes the Insurgents prisoner (chap. 13).

Scylsday
Shadeup Viron forms new government, declaring Silk caldé.
7:00 a.m. Prisoners put onto airship (chap. 14).
8:00 a.m. Hammerstone and Sand at Ermine's take Siyuf and Violet hostage to exchange for Silk and Marble (chap. 14). Mucor possesses Saba, orders airship to head east (chap. 14). It goes east for an hour (chap. 14).
3:00 p.m. Second Siyuf (chem) revealed (chap. 14).
4:00 p.m. Silk and Horn on gondola roof (chap. 15). Kypris's temptation of Silk (chap. 15).
Shadelow Airship, pushed along by strong wind, arrives at Mainframe.

Molpsday
Shadeup Auk, Chenille, Gib (and others) leave Whorl on first lander (chap. 16). Departure from Mainframe (chap. 16). Hy and Saba have sex while Horn distracts Silk (chap. 16).
3:00 p.m. Airship arrives back at Viron, where winter has hit and renewed fighting has broken out. Mint in Orilla (chap. 16). Bison about to attack (chap. 16). Silk and Hyacinth on horseback (chap. 16). The Vironese exodus begins with the people of the Sun Street quarter going into the tunnels.

APPENDIX LSA2: SELECT CHARACTERS OF THE LONG SUN

- Auk
- Chenille
- Hyacinth
- Mint
- Mucor
- Oreb
- Rose
- Silk
- Tick

Auk

An accomplished thief of Viron (I, chap. 3), Auk has straight brown hair and a reddish beard (II, chap. 7). Because Auk's face is like that of a wolf or bear, it seems to Silk that "Auk" is not his real name (I, chap. 3). That he has teeth capable of "severing a human hand at the wrist" (I, chap. 12) makes him sound like Fenris, the monster wolf of Norse myth.

There is some secret about his birth: perhaps an unknown father (I, chap. 3). He was born on Wine Street (IV, chap. 12). He cannot remember his mother Lily (III, chap. 3). His brother Bustard, possibly born in winter, was three years older (III, chap. 3) but he died.

In his bedroom, Auk has a poster of Scylla, a surprising

symbol of his religious and patriotic sentiments. Later he meets Scylla, when she is possessing Chenille. Auk offers sacrifices to Tartaros the god of thieves, which makes professional sense, but Dace says Auk belongs to Hierax, the god of death (III, chap. 1). Scylla tells Auk to convince Silk to obey her, with the contingency that if Auk cannot persuade Silk, he is to kill Silk and be her caldé himself (III, chap. 1).

As an orphan, Auk called Mint his mother, which was their secret (I, chap. 3). While trapped in the tunnels, Auk seems to send a telepathic message to Mint, asking her to send a god (III, chap. 8).

Horn's observation that "[Chenille would] be a lot like Auk if she was a man" (IV, chap. 15) suggests that Auk is another natural child of Caldé Tussah, which would make Chenille his half-sister.

Auk's character contains elements of Father Brown's thief Flambeau as well as Moses.

Chenille
A prostitute at Orchid's brothel (II, chap. 5), Chenille is one of the tallest there, second only to Violet. She is part of a spy network through Dr. Crane for Trivigaunte. Previously bedded by Colonel Oosik of Viron (III, chap. 5), she is illiterate (II, chap. 1).

Chenille kills Orpine (possessed by Mucor) while intoxicated by rust (and also possessed by Mucor?), supposedly because Mucor/Orpine made a lewd homosexual proposition.

Kypris possesses Chenille at Orpine's funeral. Her subsequent dagger-throw attests to goddess skills (II, chap. 4). But later Chenille thinks Auk loves the Kypris in her, not knowing the real Chenille at all (III, chap. 3).

Scylla possesses Chenille at the Lake Shrine (II, chap. 13). In seizing a boat, she gouges a man's eyes and strikes with her left hand first (II, chap. 11).

The Trivigaunte Generalissimo Siyuf beds her at Ermine's (IV, chap. 11); Chenille, who claimed to have killed Orpine over a lewd proposition, is no longer squeamish about homosexual activity, or perhaps it is the Kypris in her. This action finds a strong parallel with that of Saba and Hyacinth on the airship.

It turns out that Chenille is Caldé Tussah's natural daughter. She is last seen on the first lander with Auk, Gib, and the other thieves of Auk's knot, bound for planet Green.

Hyacinth
A prostitute who resides at Blood's villa, Hyacinth is the owner of both the azoth and the needler that Silk acquires (I, chap. 6). Hy has green eyes (I, chap. 12), black hair (I, chap. 6), and large breasts. She usually cries before sleep and sometimes during sleep (IV, chap. 11).

Hy was born on the east side of Viron, and there is another woman at Orchid's, Poppy, from the same quarter (II, chap. 5). Hy's father is a head clerk at the Juzgado (II, chap. 5), and she has a low opinion of him, saying, "he's a pig's arse" (IV, chap. 3).

At age 14 Hy was seduced by a commissioner (probably Simuliid or Trematode), then she lived for a while with Captain Serval, "but there was some sort of trouble.... Then she came to Orchid's" (II, chap. 5).

When Hyacinth became a prostitute at Orchid's place, she was flat-chested before she met Dr. Crane (II, chap. 5). Hy and Chenille fought with fists twice: Chen says she won the first time but Hy paid her back (IV, chap. 15). Hy is secretive about this with Silk, which has a curious link to the scene at the Sun Street manteion arbor (II, chap. 5) where Chenille, ridden by Kypris (III, chap. 4), tells Silk and Auk how much she likes Hyacinth (II, chap. 5).

Hy left Orchid's a couple weeks after Chenille moved in (II, chap. 5), taking up residence at Blood's villa, where Colonel Oosik bedded her and perhaps fell in love with her (III, chap. 8).

Hy's relationship with Kypris is complicated. Silk wonders about the Kypris in Hy: "Had Kypris possessed Hyacinth, rendering her irresistible? Could she possess two women simultaneously?" (III, chap. 8).

Hy's shrine for Kypris at Blood's villa (IV, chap. 11) makes it seem as though she needs Kypris possession like a drug: that is why she is so desperate to get back to the villa. Once she gets there, Hy cries in the ruins of her room (IV, chap. 11). Perhaps rust addiction is just a cover for possession-addiction, making Hyacinth a little puppet goddess who has to merge with the big one at regular intervals to remain functional. This might be the real reason she refuses to leave the Whorl at the exodus: that she reasonably fears she would be cut off from the necessary technology (Sacred Windows and glasses) that allows her access to Kypris.

Perhaps Hy is always possessed by Kypris when we see her in the text. Oosik sends her away but she jumps onto the moving floater with goddess agility (III, chap. 9). Hy talks about taking sword-fighting lessons from Xiphias (IV, chap. 11), yet she uses the same "thumbs into eyes" maneuver that Scylla used while riding Chenille (IV, chap. 15). When Horn on top of the gondola uses the analogy that Hyacinth is like Mucor's lynxes, bad to others yet loving to Silk (IV, chap. 15), the analogy backfires outside of the text since Silk knows that he is not the master of Hyacinth; Kypris is. In this sense of long-term possession, Hyacinth might be similar to Maytera Rose, who seems to be possessed by Echidna.

On the airship Hyacinth has sex with General Saba (IV, chap. 16). Presumably this is to curry favor with their new jailer, but at the same time it strongly echoes the trysting between Chenille and Siyuf, and Violet and Siyuf, with its hint of goddesses at play.

Some actions are more mysterious or simply capricious, as when Hy applies makeup to match the face on her wedding ring (IV, chap. 12).

In her scarlet dress, Hyacinth resembles the Whore of Babylon from the Bible's Book of Revelation.

Mint

At thirty-six years old (II, chap. 5), Mint is the youngest sibyl of the Sun Street manteion, and she has been a sibyl for twenty years (III, chap. 9). The fact that Brocket is a distant cousin is a possible hint for her birth name. When Auk was younger, he pretended that Mint was his mother, and she knows it. She never had an older sister, but she considered Maytera Mockorange as one.

Mint accidentally traps a piece of Kypris within her by closing her eyes during a theophany before Kypris could get back out. Perhaps because of her being touched by a goddess, Mint exhibits new mental powers. Fatigued on the streets, she uses a dream-like telepathy to talk with Auk in the tunnels (III, chap. 5), and later she does it again when she is underground and he is above ground (IV, chap. 6).

Mint's transformation into a military genius turns her into a Joan of Arc.

There are strong parallels between Mint and Marble, in that both start the series as sibyls and end by becoming laywomen for love. But note that while there are two passages in *Exodus from the Long Sun* (IV, chap. 14, p. 313 and chap. 17, p. 380) that suggest Mint merging with Marble and Marble merging with Mint, seemingly foreshadowed by an earlier passage (II, chap. 8, p. 208), they are actually typos according to Wolfe in a postal interview.

Mucor
The "daughter" of Blood (I, chap. 5), Mucor is actually a cold one brought to term in a surrogate mother (perhaps Orchid). Silk says she is one of Molpe's children, meaning that she is insane (I, chap. 5), but he may be literally correct. Later, Silk says she is Hierax's child (III, chap. 2). Hierax is one of the few things, if not the only thing, Mucor is afraid of (II, chap. 9).

Mucor says the lynxes are her children, and she did give birth to them (I, chap. 5).

Mucor can leave her body to search around and possess people, but torturing her body brings her back to it (III, chap. 7).

Mucor is a darker version of Thuvia, maid of Mars in the Barsoom series by Edgar Rice Burroughs.

Oreb

Silk's night chough (I, chap. 2), Oreb is said to be from the swamps of Palustria. Since Palustria is also the origin for the brain surgeon who "accidentally" damaged Mucor, and with the evidence of Oreb's power of speech, obviously the Palustrians have some biomedical or bioengineering skill. Oreb might be an espionage agent of Palustria. He might be an oracle of a god, at two points (IV, chap. 11 and chap. 14), Tick says of Oreb, "Add cot!" which might mean "Bad god!"

Oreb calls Quetxal "Bad thing" (III, chap. 8). He seems able to see that Quetzal is an inhumu.

Rose

The senior sibyl at Sun Street manteion until her death (II, chap. 11), Rose is around 90 years old, at least (I, chap. 9), and she served the manteion for 60-odd years. Her nose, mouth, and right eye are polymer (I, chap. 2). She has two prosthetic arms, after a strange disease took her arms when she was in her forties. She seems to also have prosthetic legs, and some devices in her chest, including her larynx (I, chap. 2).

Rose's terrible secret is about Blood, her son by Pike (III, chap. 4). Rose was 40 years old at the time of his birth. She believes that Echidna blinded her and took her arms as punishment for her fornication with Pike.

Rose visited Blood and his foster mother once each season, until she lost track of the foster mother when he was nine years old (III, chap. 10). In Blood's version, his biological mother visited a few times when he was little.

Because Rose lost her arms, she is a living version of Venus de Milo, the famous armless statue that is a Wolfe trope.

Speculatively, the clues can be assembled into a story of a "love nest" of the gods. That is, it seems likely that Rose was possessed by Kypris, and Pike was possessed by Pas, and they enjoyed carnal relations. Pas rewarded Pike with a visit (I, chap. 2), but when Echidna found out, she punished Rose by removing her arms and taking up full-time residence within her. Rose's glass remained functional while Pike's broke down (III, chap. 4).

Silk
The hero, Silk is an augur enlightened by the Outsider on the ball court of the first page. He is 23 years old. He is tall, with blond hair and blue eyes, in contrast to his mother who was small and dark (I, chap. 7).

Of his early life, there was the year he and his mother had gone to the country for no reason (II, chap. 4). At age 12, he required glasses to read (I, chap. 4), and on one occasion he broke into a deserted house (I, chap. 5).

His mother wanted him in politics, to become a clerk (like Hyacinth's father) and perhaps rise to commissioner (III, chap. 10). Despite this, Silk chose instead to become an augur. He spent eight years at schola (I, chap. 2) but his (foster/surrogate) mother died before he was assigned to the Sun Street manteion (I, chap. 1). In fact, he had been at schola for six years when she died (II, chap. 1).

Silk came to assist Patera Pike, but Pike died after the first year, leaving Silk as leader of the place. At the start of the series, he has been there about two years.

Xiphias surmises Silk is left handed in combat, which is news to Silk.

Silk has many features of a sacred king: "virgin" birth, foster mother, hidden identity as heir to the throne, secret flight from homeland, and lamed (while escaping Hyacinth). He also wrestles "Death" and wins, obtains a magic sword, rides toward the capital city on a white donkey, dies and is revived (a few times at least).

There is a suggestion that Caldé Tussah sought a cold one (frozen embryo) to use as an heir or a weapon (II, chap. 7). Silk shows signs of being a genetically engineered vengeance weapon for Pas, in that he is a fighting machine who is so loyal that he would never usurp the throne, a "Horus device" to be used if a revolt in Mainframe deposes Pas.

Silk has elements of Father Brown, Moses, Aaron, and Jesus.

Tick

The catachrest Silk rejected before buying Oreb (IV, character list), Tick's name is a catachrestic substitution for the word "talk," in addition to being a homonym for a vocal "tic."

As a talking cat, Tick is perceived by at least one Trivigaunti as being an oracle of Sphigx. Tick seems to admit this is true: "Hat's shoe!" (IV, chap. 14).

APPENDIX LSA3: THE LONG SUN AND THE BOOK OF EXODUS

The life of Moses has a number of iconic scenes, the top five being: the baby Moses in the bullrushes; the burning bush; the "Set my people free" scene; the parting of the Red Sea; and the receiving of the Ten Commandments.

Wolfe avoids all of these. Once he lights the "Exodus" sign in the title of the fourth book, then it is off to the races, yet using some of the lesser episodes:

Pharaoh's slaughter of the newborns is turned into the governmental search among the children for an heir.

Moses's being raised by a secret foster mother becomes Silk being raised by a secret foster mother.

Moses's killing of an Egyptian is turned into Auk kicking a man to death.

Moses's being called upon by God becomes Silk's enlightenment on the ball court and later his first view outside the Long Sun Whorl.

The monotheism of Moses becomes the semi-monotheism of Silk.

Moses discovering his brother Aaron and sister Miriam is turned into Silk discovering his brother Auk and sister Chenille.

The Ten Plagues of Egypt is downgraded to a single mention of plagues in prophecy of the Chrasmologic Writings.

The jewelry taken from the Egyptians is translated as the Kypris heist.

The leader of the evacuation is a role taken by Auk.

The jewelry sacrificed on Mount Horeb becomes the need to repair landers with cards.

The brazen serpent miracle is used for the enigmatic Quetzal resting in his tree and healing victims of snake-bite.

That Moses and Aaron are forbidden to enter the Promised Land becomes Silk, Auk, and Quetzal being denied access to Blue.

In addition to all the Moses material, Jesus points keep showing up, bringing New Testament elements to the mix.

The miraculous conception of Jesus becomes the cold one implantation of Silk.

Silk and his mother leaving town for a year, to avoid the governmental search mentioned above, looks more like the holy family's Flight to Egypt.

Jesus entering Jerusalem in triumph becomes Silk touring Viron as caldé.

Judas betraying Jesus is turned into Urus selling out Spider.

Jesus and Peter in Gethsemane becomes Mint and Auk in the Grand Manteion.

The Holy Spirit resurrecting Jesus after three days is translated into Auk resurrecting Sand after three naps.

"Love is patient . . ." becomes Silk's mini-sermon to Horn about Hyacinth.

Revelation's Whore of Babylon is linked to Hyacinth, for her profession, her scarlet dress, et cetera.

Thus, the pattern of mixing Old Testament and New Testament elements established by the first text given from the Chrasmologic Writings, "Are ten birds to be had for a song? You have daubed Oreb the raven, but can you make him sing?" (I, chap. 2), is maintained throughout the Long Sun series.

APPENDIX LSA4: OF THE GODS (I)

On the Long Sun Whorl, a family of monsters (including a sea monster, a Siren, and a Sphinx) have been set up as gods. They start out in a Greco-Roman "Mount Olympus" scenario, a household headed by a philandering patriarch. Things change when the mother of monsters leads a rebellion and kills her husband in a mashup of the murder of Agamemnon in Greek legend and the murder and reconstruction of the god Osiris in Egyptian mythology.

Those loyal to Pas include Kypris, goddess of love, and Tartaros, god of thieves. One detail that Wolfe might be playing off here is that Kypris is associated with Venus, Tartaros is associated with Mercury, and the planets Venus and Mercury are both "morning/evening stars," for being closer to the Sun.

Sun: Pas (controller of the long sun)
Mercury: Tartaros, god of thieves
Venus: Kypris, goddess of love
Earth: Echidna, goddess of motherhood
Mars: Sphigx, goddess of war
Jupiter: Pas-as-philanderer
Saturn: The Outsider
Uranus: (discovered 1781, not among the family)
Neptune: (1846) Scylla, goddess of waters
Pluto: (1930–2006) Hierax, god of death

The Outsider has two attributes linking him to Saturn the planet and Saturn the god. For the ancient world (indeed, until fairly recently) the planet Saturn was the outermost one, the outsider. Even before heliocentric orbits were known and calculated, the planet was named after an older god, a pre-Olympian who had been cast into the outer darkness by the victorious new gods. The god Saturn is associated with crows, just as the Outsider is.

The Outsider has details linking him to Jesus and God the Father. The tale of the Outsider beating the animal sellers (I, chap. 1, 17) echoes the episode of Jesus and the Money Changers (Mark 11: 17). The execution of a criminal (II, chap. 11, 285) links to the crucifixion of Jesus. Elements pointing to God the Father include the passage of sacred text claiming that the Outsider created man from mud (II, chap. 5, 111); the statement that Ah Lah ("Allah") is another name for the Outsider; and Silk's vision by the fish pool, where the Outsider claims Kypris because love always proceeds from him (III, chap. 7, 266).

BIBLIOGRAPHY FOR THE LONG SUN

Aurelius, Marcus. *The Meditations.* AD 167. (III, chap. 2)
The Bible. Exodus (IV, title; IV, chap. 2; IV, chap. 4; IV, chap. 16)
———. Deuteronomy (IV, My Defense)
———. 1 Samuel (IV, chap. 12)
———. Job (I, chap. 2)
———. Psalms (IV, chap. 8)
———. Matthew (I, chap. 2; IV, chap. 11; IV, chap. 12)
———. Mark (I, chap. 1; III, chap. 3)
———. Romans (IV, chap. 12)
———. 1 Corinthians (IV, chap. 16)
———. 1 Peter (IV, chap. 12)
———. Revelation (III, chap. 9)
Bismarck, Otto von. Quote "Fools learn from experience . . ." (II, chap. 9)
Bouvier, John. *Bouvier's Law Dictionary.* (BLD). 1865.
Burroughs, Edgar Rice. *The Gods of Mars.* 1913. (I, chap. 5)
Carroll, Lewis. *Alice's Adventures in Wonderland.* 1865. (IV, chap. 1)
Chace, Howard L. "Laddle Rat Rotten Hut." 1940. (I, chap. 2)
Chesterton, G. K. "The Blue Cross." 1910. (I, chap. 12)
———. *The Man Who Was Thursday.* 1908. (Appendix L1A2)
Dick, Philip K. *Do Androids Dream of Electric Sheep?* 1968. (II, chap. 11)
Heifetz, Josefa. *Mrs. Byrne's Dictionary.* 1974.

Hendin, David. *Guide to Biblical Coins.* (I, chap. 2)
Oxford English Dictionary (OED).
Virgil. *The Aeneid.* 19 BC. (II, chap. 7; IV, chap. 1)
Wolfe, Gene. *Castle of Days.* 1992. (IV, Dedication)

INTERLUDE: "THE NIGHT CHOUGH"

A story first published in *The Crow: Shattered Lives and Broken Dreams* (1998), "The Night Chough" was collected in *Innocents Aboard* (2004).

Oreb is apparently on planet Blue, at a human colony that uses naming conventions from Viron. The bird finds the corpse of Lily in the water of a pond and its attempt to eat the body activates a fragment of goddess Scylla within Oreb.

A young man named Starling comes along, searching for the corpse. He talks to the bird about how Moonrat and Caracal told him that his beloved Lily was raped and murdered by Serval, Bushdog, and Marten the day before. He then seeks vengeance.

It is raining when Starling uses his fishing gaff to pull Marten through a house window and to his death. Starling is surprised the others in the house do not emerge to kill him.

At a tavern, Starling enters to provoke expulsion for himself and Bushdog. He succeeds and waits in the rain. Moonrat suddenly appears and gives Starling a slug gun, a rifle. Bushdog comes out and claims Serval was the killer. Starling, regretting his ambush of Marten, fights Bushdog on even terms and, with some help from Oreb, kills him with his bare hands.

Afterward Moonrat catches up and leads him to Serval's location. Along the way, Moonrat sees Scylla walking beside Starling.

They extract Serval from his house. Starling demands that

Serval help bury Lily.

First they must fish her out. At the pond, Starling keeps the rifle ready and has Moonrat give the gaff to Serval. Oreb helpfully indicates where the body is. Serval wades out and stirs the water until lightning strikes a dead tree nearby, when Serval flees in terror. Starling shoots in the dark. Moonrat says he hit, and offers to go finish him off. Starling disarms Moonrat and tells him to get Lily's corpse.

When the corpse is on the bank, and Moonrat is back in the pond, Starling urges Moonrat to confess to the rape and murder. Moonrat denies it. Starling assembles the clues that have come up. They have a showdown and Starling shoots him dead.

Observation: This story provides the first glimpse of life on Blue. The mystery-solving side that shows up near the end is congruent with the detective threads in the Long Sun books. The theme of violence and revenge, while a perfect fit for an anthology on "The Crow" franchise, initially seems distant from the Long Sun series, until one recalls the "War in Mainframe" level, which is about a murder (of Pas) and the revenge that follows.

One surprise is the revelation that Oreb is being ridden by the goddess Scylla, at least at the time of this story. This seems to give the answer to a riddle between Oreb and Tick the catachrest, who had seemingly said that Oreb was a bad god, without naming that god, and then Tick admitted to being ridden by Sphigx. It also seems related to how "Oreb" is substituted for "Leviathan" in the Bible quote in notes for volume I, chapter 2: there was a hint from the first appearance of the name "Oreb."

But the Scylla in this story seems different from the Scylla seen on Sacred Windows and in possessed Chenille; this Scylla seems to be avenging, rather than self-serving. Or maybe that is too charitable, and this Scylla is using the excuse of revenge to rack up more human sacrifices to herself, especially those killings at the pond.

ON BLUE'S WATERS

(Volume V)

Edition cited: Tor (hb), ISBN 978-0-3128-6614-3, 1999, 381 pp.

Dedication: "Respectfully dedicated to Roy and Matt."
　Commentary: Wolfe's sons Roy Emerson II (named after Wolfe's father) and Matthew Dietsch. Roy passed away in 2017, preceding his father by two years.

[Preface] To Every Town (13)

An open letter from a town named Pajarocu, calling on colonists interested in an expedition across space to revisit the Long Sun Whorl.
　Observation: The naming conventions ("He-hold-fire") and the metaphors ("rise upon fire and fly like the eagle") used in the letter sound primitive to the point of stone age, leading the reader to wonder how far down the technology ladder the colonists have fallen.
　Literary: Jack London's "The Strength of the Strong" (1911) comes to mind as a post-apocalyptic caveman story, with characters named "Lip-King," "Long Beard," "Deer-Runner," and "Afraid-of-the-Dark."

1. Horn's Book (17–48)

(Horn begins haltingly. He writes about the pen case.) [Frame tale synopsis to be given within parentheses.]

* * * [Asterisks denote text breaks.]

(He is in Gaon, a land-locked town of Blue. He has searched three worlds for Silk, and though he has failed to find him, he continues still, now sending out letters. Oreb had been with him, but is gone now.)

* * *

Horn sets the beginning at the day a large boat visited his island off the coast. Relations with his elder son Sinew were strained. The boat brought the five faction leaders of New Viron. They need a caldé for New Viron, and they want Silk. The most recent lander came from Old Viron sixteen years before.

They show Horn the letter from Pajarocu.

* * *

(In the frame tale at Gaon, Horn and his helper Hari Mau have formalized the law court system.)

After the five leave, Horn discusses the situation with his family. It has to do with the failing crops, and the method to maintain good crops requires regular cross-breeding.

They note "conjunction" is coming, with an invasion of inhumi. Horn will go to get Silk and corn.

* * *

Horn describes Lizard Island. He and Nettle came to Blue twenty years before.

* * *

(In Gaon he listens to court cases.)

Horn gives Sinew his needler. Conjunction in two years.

* * *

Horn jumps ahead to Marrow showing him a boat.

(Horn writes that Silk has become a mythic figure.)

* * *

(Horn names the readers he hopes for.)

***

(In Gaon he thinks on land reform.)

Horn leaves that night, sailing down the coast toward New Viron.

***

Horn reflects on the enormity of his quest.

Culture: Gaon seems to have a Hindu culture: "Gaon" means "village"; "Hari Mau" can mean "Chief Hari"; "Nadi" means "river"; "Nauvan" means "ninth"; "Somvar" means "Monday."

Observation: This narrative is certainly beginning "in the middle of things," in that the narrator seems to have failed his quest but has not yet returned home.

The opening has such melancholy, such grim sadness. Horn's domestic life is roiling with father/son tension. The spiritual life is crippled since the colonists have left the land of their technology-dependent gods. The grind of adult life has Horn write, "What would I not give to be the boy I was once more?" (34). Where "The Book of Silk" begins with Silk's enlightenment, "The Book of Horn" starts with Horn's malaise.

Technology: Horn and Sinew are very concerned about technological slippage, which builds upon the theme in the letter suggesting stone-age. That is, Viron had declined to 19th century technology by the time New Viron was founded, and now the stone age bow and arrow technology is looking to replace the slug gun technology.

Long Sun Whorl hints: Horn writes about the pen case, the ashes of the shop, and Oreb (17); he also has Hyacinth's azoth (44).

Green hints: Horn mentions that his son Sinew is on Green (27; 41).

Pig notes: Horn introduces a new character who is blind (33).

Bringing Great Pas: Sinew's insight (35; 38).

2. Becalmed (49–68)

Drifting in the water, lacking wind, Horn begins to re-read his book, *The Book of the Long Sun.* He thinks on developing printing press technology. He thinks on the gods.

* * *

(Horn paints one of the lenses of his eyeglasses.)
Horn ponders the gods some more.

* * *

He jumps ahead to a conversation with Remora.

* * *

Horn jumps ahead to say his prayer was answered by a leatherskin.

He prays to whatever god might hear. A leatherskin comes, a monster with claws. Horn harpoons it, and it tows him a bit before cutting the line. Then a breeze comes.

* * *

(In Gaon, Horn thinks on ways he might escape his gracious hosts and return to New Viron. He reveals they have made him their ruler, giving him fifteen young wives.)

Biographical: Nettle writing out copies of his words (50) is not only Wolfe imagining the labor of a small press spouse, but also the autobiographical detail of Wolfe's wife Rosemary writing out her favorite passages of his writings as a personal gift that would become *Gene Wolfe's Orbital Thoughts* (1992).

Prester John: The situation in Gaon starts to sound like the legendary kingdom of Prester John.

Plato's Cave: "Silk said once that we are like a man who can see only shadows, and thinks the shadow of an ox the ox and a man's shadow the man" (V, chap. 2, 49).   One of the powerful touchstones of the Long Sun series is the way that the situation on the Long Sun Whorl matches Plato's analogy of the cave. Plato said that all people are in a cave, facing the back wall where they see shadows, and they confuse these shadows for reality. One man is able to escape the cave and see reality, thereby becoming a philosopher, and then he returns to tell the others.

In *The Book of the Long Sun,* this breakthrough starts with Silk's enlightenment (I, chap. 1), but then hits a more literal point when he looks outside his "cave" of the Whorl to see space and stars outside (II, chap. 10). The implication is that the Long Sun Whorl, gods are all false and the Outsider is true.

3. The Sibyl and the Sorceress (69–94)

At New Viron, Horn meets with Marrow. Marrow lets him take a slug gun. Marrow has a slave, and this fact bothers Horn.

* * *

Horn jumps ahead to mention an incident on Green, where he met a man who could not see the inhumi.

When Horn returns to the sloop, he finds he has been robbed.

* * *

After a while he sets out, going south along the coast. Remora had avoided his questions about Marble and Mucor, but Marrow had told what little he knew. With two days of sailing, he arrives at their island.

* * *

(In Gaon, Horn makes fresh ink in order to continue his writing.)

Horn meets Mucor and Marble. He gives them food. Mucor sends him down to the landing for three live fish, then Mucor goes into a trance to find Silk on the Long Sun Whorl. Marble gives Horn one of her blind eyes in case he can find another one. Marble reads his future in a fish, and at the sacrifice Horn feels the presence of the Outsider. After this, Horn sleeps on his sloop.

* * *

(Horn ponders the prophecy, and the mystery of the three fish.)

Unusual Terms and Phrases

Hus—(Greek) pig.

Barsoom: The hus has eight limbs, which recalls the multi-limbed nature of Barsoomian creatures, where the lion and the dog have ten limbs, the horse has eight, and the ape has six.

Myth: Even though Horn knew Marble and Mucor in his childhood, his consulting them at the start of his quest seems just like a hero of ancient Greece seeking guidance from the Oracle.

Observation: With regard to Mucor, notice that her spiritual transit to the Long Sun Whorl is not instantaneous; after perhaps an hour, Marble says she doubts if Mucor has arrived there yet.

Green hints: Horn met a man who could not see the inhumi (74); Horn was riding a three-horned beast at the time he was fatally wounded (94).

Long Sun Whorl hints: At Ermine's, Horn dreamed he had killed Silk (74).

4. The Tale of the Pajarocu (95–122)

The next morning, he visits the two. Mucor is out of her trance: the good news is that she found Silk; the bad news is that Silk asked her not to tell Horn where he is.

Horn admits that his *The Book of the Long Sun* has caused this desire for Silk as ruler in many cities, not just New Viron. He also tells them of Marrow's slave, and the other slaves in New Viron. Horn gives them his copy of the book; in response, Mucor sends her hus Babbie to go with him.

* * *

(Storm hits Gaon.)
Babbie arrives on the sloop and they dislike each other.

* * *

(In Gaon a captured inhuma is buried alive.)
Back at New Viron, Horn looks up a merchant for information on Pajarocu. They share a meal at Marrow's house. Wijzer is from Dorp. He tells the legend of Pajarocu, an invisible bird that always moves around. Wijzer draws him a map to the area of the western continent where the town of Pajarocu migrates.

Observation: Marble's blindness is like Rose being struck blind after having Blood.

Odyssey: Mucor giving Horn an intelligent pig makes her

somewhat similar to Circe, who famously turned men into pigs. Circe eventually helped Odysseus in his adventure.

Myth: In Mexican folklore, Pajaro Cu (the Coo Bird). This bird named Cu had no feathers, and he was engaged to be married to the dove. The ground owl took up a collection and each bird donated a feather to clothe Cu, but when he was dressed, Cu flew away. And now the dove is always calling for him: "Cu, cu."

Green hints: Geier said inhumi are like slugs and leeches (109).

5. The Thing on the Green Plain (123–46)

Horn writes about Wijzer.

* * *

(Horn comments on the accusation that his *The Book of the Long Sun* was a fiction.)

Horn and Babbie sleep on the sloop at dock.

* * *

(In Gaon the Green-driven storms are growing worse.)

Horn and Babbie sail the next day at shadeup. They pass Lizard. They sail up the coast for weeks.

* * *

(In Gaon, a visitor gives Horn a book.)

(Editorial comments by Hoof and Hide, Daisy and Vadsig.)

The sailing idyl and thoughts on the settling of Blue.

* * *

The idyl is altered by a pirate ship, and Horn starts his western crossing much earlier than he had planned.

Something mysterious happens during the night, leaving traces of blood on the deck.

The next morning, they come to a low island.

* * *

Horn jumps ahead to an episode of Seawrack and the shaman.

They spend the day crossing seaweed, passing the island. At dusk they hear something, the Mother's song.

***

The next noon they head to the island. After searching for an hour, they leave to drift around the isle. They land at a different spot and search. They are attacked by a monster, a devil-fish.

***

(In Gaon, Horn sacrifices an elephant.)

When they return to the sloop, Seawrack is there.

6. Seawrack (147–70)

(In Gaon, ambassadors from Skany arrive, saying they heard Silk was ruling Gaon, and they invite Horn to rule Skany, too.)

Horn meets Seawrack. She dives into the water and disappears for hours. The Mother, a sea goddess, brings her back.

***

Horn retells seeing Seawrack for the first time, then to seeing the Mother, and jumps forward to Quadrifons. He ponders the gods.

***

(Horn travels from Gaon to Skany, staying there most of the summer, before returning to Gaon.)

***

In the night a storm comes and blows the sloop. The green island rips in half, being a plant form in ocean shallows. A crabman monster comes onboard, a sort of immortalized one of the Vanished People, and then it departs.

Seawrack requests one of the rings and Horn puts it on her finger.

***

They continue west, crossing the sea. They meet a ship from Dorp, learn about an island to the west with good water.

***

(Horn re-reads this chapter and comments on it with dismay.)

Arabian Nights: The growing tide of Homer's *Odyssey,* with Horn as the sailing hero who meets a Siren, develops an Arabian

Nights current with the arrival of the Mother, the tearing of the island, and the strange visit by the crabman monster. The unusual island is much like the whale-back isle in the First Voyage of Sinbad.

Long Sun Whorl hints: mention of Quadrifons, Olivine's god (157).

Green hints: Horn fighting inhumi and their slaves on Green, fighting the settlers, fighting his own son (170).

Seawrack Singing Now: Horn in Gaon hears her (170).

7. The Island (171–90)

(In Gaon, Horn says he is a sort of fake Silk.)

* * *

That night, Krait the inhumu visits the sloop.

Horn ponders the mysteries of inhumi, conjunctions, and Patera Quetzal's presence on the Long Sun Whorl.

* * *

Horn reflects upon the inhumi and Quetzal.

* * *

Horn considers the mystery of Seawrack and the Mother.

* * *

They find the island.

* * *

They explore it and seek a high point to find their way back to the sloop.

Green hints: "On Green one finds trees . . ." (188–89).

8. The End (191–94)

Horn and Seawrack discover a circular valley that is the ruins of an ancient construction. Horn is intrigued; Seawrack is frightened. Horn manages to fall into a pit.

Long Sun Whorl hints: The pen case, the ashes of the shop (194).

9. Krait (195–224)

Horn fades in and out of consciousness, sleeping for at least three days.

Krait visits, leaves.

* * *

The next day, Horn licks the dew and is visited by a strange creature, then he has a ghostly visit with Nettle.

The next day, in the late afternoon, Krait visits a second time. They bargain, and ultimately Horn gives him the key to his house.

* * *

(In Gaon, a fortune teller tells his prediction for Horn's life [211].)

* * *

(A court case involving a man seeking protection from the Vanished People.)

* * *

On the walk back to the sloop, Horn nearly shoots Babbie, saved by Krait's slapping the rifle. Babbie charges Krait, who flies and disappears.

* * *

(Horn went in hunting party for sacred cattle.)

* * *

(Background to domestication of higher animals.)

It is night when Horn and Babbie get to the sloop. The next morning, Krait shows up and offers to lead Horn to Seawrack.

* * *

(Horn explains his use of "three whorls" [221], the "* * *" marking, representing the Long Sun Whorl, the planet Blue, and the planet Green.)

(Horn recalls a song they marched to when he was a teen in the strife of Viron.)

(Horn has time with wife Chandi.)

* * *

(Horn has dream that Oreb is back, and other events.)

Bible: When Krait says to Horn in the pit, "Those who cling to life lose it; those who fling their lives away save them" (211), this is ominous. There are similar lines at Matthew 10:39 and John 12: 25, but at Matthew 16, this comes immediately after Jesus calls on his followers to each take up his cross:

> *Then Jesus said to His disciples, "If anyone wants to come after Me, he must deny himself, take up his cross, and follow Me. For whosoever will save his life shall lose it: and whosoever will lose his life for my sake shall find it"* (Matthew 16:24–25) KJV

Song: Horn gives a verse from a marching song, beginning "Trampin'..."

> *Trampin' outwards from the city,*
> *No more lookin' than was she,*
> *'Twas there I spied a garden pretty*
> *A fountain and an apple tree.*
> *These fair young girls live to deceive you,*
> *Sad experience teaches me.*

This song seems to be Wolfe's version of an Irish folk song called variously "Spanish Lady," "Dublin City," or "Wheel of Fortune." All the songs describe the young man seeing a beautiful young woman as he passes by her dwelling place at various times of day and night, and his falling in love with her.

The first verse of "Spanish Lady" goes something like this:

> *As I walked down thro' Dublin City*
> *At the hour of twelve in the night,*
> *Who should I see but a Spanish lady*
> *Washing her feet by candlelight.*

Wolfe follows this context-setting pattern, but changes it into a "marching through the countryside" song, where the singer first chances upon a garden by a house. Then there is the line "Sad experience teaches me," which is found in a chorus of "Dublin City" (1945) by Burl Ives and "Dublin City" (1975) by Gordon Bok.

> *Round and round the wheel of fortune*
> *Where it stops wearies me*
> *Fair maids they are so deceiving*
> *Sad experience teaches me.*

Green hints: Horn writes that his spirit had gone and left his body unoccupied on Green (195); another time, lying beside dead Krait (224); the sewer (224).

Long Sun Whorl hints: Horn has a dream involving bits from his time with Pig and Oreb (223–24).

10. Seawrack's Ring (225–53)

(In Gaon, Horn goes hunting with a group, this time for killing.)

* * *

They sail in the fog, directed by Krait, and Horn hears Seawrack singing long before he sees her. She has become semi-feral, and Krait tells Horn that to win her back he must hold her close and make her sing for him.

* * *

(Horn admits he was going to omit the next episode.)

* * *

Horn makes her sing. She sings a few notes and Horn rapes her. He passes out; she bandages up and hides onboard until dark.

* * *

Then she comes out and they make up.

* * *

(In Gaon they bury an inhumu and two inhumas.)

* * *

Horn and Seawrack see fires on the coast of the western

continent. They talk in the dark.

***

(The date is Dursa Agast. Conjunction is past.)

Horn wakes up in the night and they talk. When he wakes up at dawn, she is gone.

***

(Rainy day at court.)

Horn waits around all day and at shadelow Seawrack drives a fish onboard. She gives him an ancient silver ring, and he puts it on.

Unusual Terms and Phrases

Dursa Agast—the second of August.

Observation: Driving fish is a skill Seawrack has, suggesting that she was the one who compelled the three fish Mucor spoke of, which in turn suggests some sort of communication between Mucor and Seawrack, or between Mucor and the Mother. The exchange of rings seems like a marriage ceremony. This notion retrospectively casts the crabman as a sort of priest beginning the wedding ritual of unknown stages.

Odyssey: The rape of Seawrack is a brutal version of Odysseus being tempted by the Sirens in Book XII.

Long Sun Whorl hints: "Pig would advise me" (234).

Seawrack Singing Now: Horn writes to Nettle that he will return to her, yet when he hears the song, he will leave her for his own death (240).

Green hints: "[T]he ring would save my life on Green" (253).

11. The Land of Fires (255–82)

The group lands on the western continent. Horn, Seawrack, and Babbie go west towards where Krait had fed the night before. Horn says he thinks the campfires they saw the night before were not made by humans. At noon they reach the little river and follow it.

***

It is nearly dark when they reach the family of four, led by He-pen-sheep. They refer to Neighbors being in the area, the ones at the fires.

* * *

While the others sleep, Horn sneaks off to explore.

* * *

(In Gaon, Horn visits a house of the Vanished People. He finds a chalice.)

* * *

After three or four hours, Horn hangs up his slug gun and falls asleep. He is awakened by a tall figure, a Neighbor, and follows him to a fire. They talk with him, giving humanity the planet Blue, asking permission to visit it from time to time. He agrees three times.

* * *

Heading back, he meets Babbie, and both meet a great beast, a breakbull. Horn shoots it dead. The family helps process it and they all carry meat back to the sloop.

* * *

They sail north a bit, then land to collect more green shoots with which to smoke the meat. This takes most of the day and they sleep on the sloop. Krait is absent for his watch and the sloop gets into difficulty, nearly sinking.

They see He-pen-sheep on the shore with the breakbull head, and Horn accepts it.

History: Echoes of Tierra del Fuego. In 1520, Ferdinand Magellan was the first European to see this area at the tip of South America, and he named it "land of fires" for all the mysterious campfires he saw.

Biblical: Philistines, but ones gifting the land rather than fighting.

Observation: He-pen-sheep, recognizing Horn's ring as a thing of the Neighbors, assumes that Horn became a "Neighbor-man" (262) by changing blood with a Neighbor (263), just as he had changed blood with a shearbear (261). Horn does not comment, presumably because the Neighbor ring was given to him by Seawrack rather than a Neighbor, but this blood-ritual sounds like an interesting interpretation of Horn's first encounter with a Neighbor, back in the pit. Later, when Horn is telling He-pen-sheep about his conversation with the Neighbors, he says, "We changed blood" (276). But He-pen-sheep might be right that the exchange happened before, recalling that Horn in the pit was declared dead by both Seawrack and Babbie, raising the likelihood that the Neighbor revived him with Neighbor blood.

12. War (283–311)

(In Gaon, Horn has been wounded in a war that has been going on for a month. It began with an engineering project to tame the Nadi's Lesser Cataracts. The Man of Han upriver requested another such channel around the Cataracts. Now Horn is suicidal, and he asked a wife to kill him [284].)

***

(Horn describes himself as a one-eyed man with white hair.)
(Gaon's forces have been pushed back again.)

***

(Horn rides elephant. Questions prisoners.)

***

(Sending men to buy supplies.)

***

(Driven back.)

***

(Interview prisoners. Ask for truce.)

***

(Horn arranges a prisoner exchange.)
They find the mouth of the river. They begin to sail up the river. Days grow into a week.

***

(In Gaon, temple bells are ringing in victory. The Han had advanced into a trap with explosive mines.)
At Wichote, the town on the river, Horn hears talk

suggesting that his son Sinew is ahead of them.

***

(In Gaon, Horn conspires with the head gardener.)

***

(Horn leads an expedition through the impenetrable forest, where his Neighbor's gift of bushwalking reawakens. They end up riding their alien elephant on a self-made charge into the Hannese rear.)

***

(Housekeeping tasks. Grain shortage ahead.)

***

(Rain continues. Horn sends a third of his troopers home for a week.)

At Wichote, Horn buys a meat pudding. That night, Krait returns from scouting ahead and says that he found Pajarocu. Krait tells him to form a plan for Seawrack.

(In Gaon, a plan to go out at night.)

Unusual Terms and Phrases

Choora—a type of Afghan knife, with a long, straight, single-edged blade.

"Elephant"—a creature of Blue with eight legs and two trunks. The two-trunk detail echoes the *bishter,* an elephantine creature of L. Sprague de Camp's planet Krishna, itself another world inspired by Barsoom.

Herodotus: The building of a canal around the cataract finds historical footing in Book II of *The Histories*, where Herodotus describes the canal around a cataract on the Nile in Egypt:

> 29. *From the city of Elephantine as one goes up the river there is country which slopes steeply; so that here one must attach ropes to the vessel on both sides, as one fastens an ox, and so make one's way onward; and if the rope break, the vessel is gone at once, carried away by the violence of the stream. Through this country it is a*

voyage of about four days in length, and in this part the Nile is winding like the river Maiander, and the distance amounts to twelve schoines, which one must traverse in this manner. Then you will come to a level plain, in which the Nile flows round an island named Tachompso.

This canal permitted water travel between Elephantine (modern Aswan) and Tachompso, a lost island of Ethiopia.

Long Sun Whorl hints: Pig's blind face as he ate soup (283); "Because I could not leave Pig blind, these people were able to bring me here" (308); "Where did I put Maytera's eye?" (310); "[A]nd the corn, where is that?" (310); "Found it . . . I put Olivine's eye in the pocket" (310).

Editorial Note: Nettle has read the book, as have Hoof and Hide (287).

Observation: In Gaon, Horn's wives Pehla and Alubukhara are with child (310).

13. Brothers (313–41)

(In Gaon, Horn throws away the last of Oreb's quills. He writes of the secret night mission, of digging up an inhuma and reviving her. Jahlee joins the party in the war against the Man of Han.)

* * *

The trip upriver from Wichote is laborious. Sinew surprises them by suddenly showing up. Horn proposes that Sinew stay with Seawrack in Wichote while Horn and Krait go in the lander. Both refuse.

* * *

(In the morning, Hari Mau talks with Horn in bed.)

Horn, Sinew, and Seawrack talk about personhood. Turns out Horn, Sinew, and Krait sound exactly alike.

Arabian Nights: Horn reviving inhumi seems like a generic demon summoning and demon binding, but more specifically it harkens to the background story in Arabian Nights about how all those jinns became imprisoned in bottles through the work of King Solomon. Most detailed in "The City of Brass," where the story begins,

> *She said, It hath reached me, O auspicious King, that when the Caliph Abd al-Malik bin Marwan sat conversing with his Grandees concerning our lord Solomon, and these noted what Allah had bestowed upon him of lordship and dominion, quoth the Commander of the Faithful, "Indeed he attained unto that whereto never attained other than he, in that he was wont to imprison Jinns and Marids and Satans in cucurbites of copper and stop them with lead and seal them with his ring."*

The subsequent expedition to find the lost City of Brass is impelled by the prospect of it having many of these sealed bottles. Indeed, the explorers find such a hoard, and bring it back to Baghdad at the end of the story:

> *Then he took the brazen vessels and opened them, cucurbite after cucurbite, whereupon the devils came forth of them, saying, "We repent, O Prophet of Allah! Never again will we return to the like of this thing; no never!" And the Caliph marvelled at this.*

Green hints: "It was not so on Green . . ." (324).

14. Pajarocu! (343–61)

(In Gaon, the war nears its end. Horn aims to escape, allowing Hari Mau to rule. That is, Horn sees his own death if Gaon wins or loses. In addition, Horn thinks it likely that the freed inhumi will turn against him.)

Horn starts with the lander, how Krait, Sinew, and Horn obtained places on it. How they brought weapons. Knowing that the ones controlling the lander were inhumi.

(Oreb returns and calls Horn "Silk.")

* * *

Horn writes about the portable city of Pajarocu. When he saw the lander, he recognized it was Auk's. He made plans to seize control of the lander.

The plan went badly. The men did not believe him and the lander continued on.

Green hints: "[T]he ancient black-bladed sword with which I cleared the sewer of corpses" (345).

Long Sun Whorl hints: "[T]he robe that Olivine stole for me . . . when I sacrificed in the Grand Manteion" (346).

Observation: A woman is bit by an inhumu while her husband is away at the drinking house, so the men are getting together to decide his punishment (353). "They're going to whip him or something" (356). This is a puzzling point of law.

15. The Last Sheets (363–70)

(Horn, Oreb, and Evensong are on the little escape boat. Horn writes about his father, whom he met again on the Long Sun Whorl, and about fathers and sons. They spend the daylight going down the river.)

Long Sun Whorl hints: "When our roads crossed again before Hari Mau . . . carried me off to Gaon, I did not even recognize [my father]" (366). "He has married a second time, and begun a new family" (366).

16. Northwest (371–81)

(Horn, at an unknown location, writes on how inhumi found them at their camp and hovered overhead.)

On the lander, Krait tells Horn to storm into the cockpit.

(Evensong asks Horn for the inhumi secret. Horn tells how the inhumi are only as intelligent as the creatures they drink from.)

(Sometime in the night, Horn leaves, following a voice in the forest.)

***

(Horn writes goodbyes; writes that he was comforted by an entity.)

***

(In the forest, Horn finds two children. He teaches them how to fish with a spear and how to trap with a cord.)

***

(Horn dreams.)

***

(Horn re-reads and comments. He tells about the fight on the lander.)

Long Sun Whorl hints: Dream involving Pig, Hound, Olivine, Hyacinth (379).

Song: A verse, beginning, "I'm old now . . ." (381).

> *I'm old now, and soon must leave you,*
> *But a fairer maid I ne'er did see.*
> *Curse me not that I bereave you*
> *I cannot stay, no more would she.*
> *These fair young girls live to deceive you,*
> *Sad experience teaches me.*

This verse, apparently a concluding verse, seems to draw from a version of "Spanish Lady" by Joseph Campbell (1879–1944):

> *Old age has laid its hand upon me*
> *Cold as a fire of ashy coal*
> *And where is the lovely Spanish Lady*
> *The maid so neat about the sole?*

Wolfe augments this weight of passing years with lines from the Burl Ives version of "Dublin City" attesting to the woman's singular beauty ("And in all my life I ne'er did see") as well as their mutual separation ("And I no more to she, nor she to me"). Wolfe also takes the "Fair maids they are so deceiving/Sad experience teaches me" from Ives and uses them for every verse.

Putting this together to show each line with a possible source:

> I'm old now, and soon must leave you, ["Spanish Lady"]
> But a fairer maid I ne'er did see. ["Dublin City"]
> Curse me not that I bereave you
> I cannot stay, no more would she. ["Dublin City"]
> These fair young girls live to deceive you, ["Dublin City"]
> Sad experience teaches me. ["Dublin City"]

APPENDICES FOR ON BLUE'S WATERS

Appendix S1A1: Timelines
Because the story begins in medias res, there are two tracks: New Viron to Green, and Gaon.

Symbols: page numbers from first edition hardcover; "~:" is used to mark a break in time of uncertain duration.

Timeline from New Viron to Green

Day: Note
1: The mainshaft of the papermill had split when Hide tells Horn a ship is coming to their island (V, chap. 1, 19). It is the five faction-leaders of New Viron—Blazingstar, Eschar, Gyrfalcon, Marrow, and Patera Remora. After they leave, Horn has dinner with his family to explain what he has sworn to do (26). Horn accepts the mission to go to the Long Sun Whorl and return with Silk to New Viron. Sinew thinks the real plan is to bring Pas to Blue (35). Conjunction with Green is due in two years (38). Horn leaves at night, while Nettle, Hoof, and Hide are asleep (42).
2: Day at sea (44), Horn prays for wind, and at sunset is visited by a leatherskin (chap. 2, 59–61).
3: New Viron. Horn talks to Remora about gods of the Vanished People (56–58). Remora flatly refuses to tell anything about Maytera Marble (chap. 3, 75).
4: Horn's ship is robbed of some valuables while he is at Marrow's (74).
5: To Mucor's Rock, two days' worth of travel (78), where

Marrow had said even with a good wind it would take all day.
6: Midmorning arrive at Rock.
7: Next morning, Mucor has returned from visiting Silk (chap. 4, 95). Gift of book for Marble, gift of Babbie for Horn. Back to New Viron, arrive in time for dinner with Wijzer at Marrow's. Horn spends night at dock. Horn's plan is to sail north 100 leagues, then cut west (122).
8: Sail at dawn (chap. 5, 126), pass Lizard after noon (127). Beginning of six weeks' sailing time (128).
50: A pirate boat gives chase (132), and Horn kills a woman shooting at him. She falls into the sea. To avoid the pirates Horn begins sailing west.
51: The next morning Horn finds blood on deck (134). Babbie gets small tree at sunset (138). They hear the Mother's song, probably sorrowing for Seawrack's wound.
52: Next dawn they find a low green island (141). Babbie had been on board for several weeks (141). Inland the great flat creature attacks them. They return to sloop to find Seawrack (145). She leaves, is brought back by the Mother (chap. 6, 152–53). Storm comes at night (160), tears up vegetative green island (161). A crustacean man thing comes on board for a tense, enigmatic encounter (161). The following days they sail west-northwest. This period includes the best and happiest hours of his life, "days of gold" spent with Seawrack (170).
~:
57: Nearly a week later (163) they meet another ship (166) and learn of a young man (Sinew) searching for Horn. Captain Strik says they should sail north by northwest for Pajarocu (167). News of an island with good water two or three days west (169). At night Krait comes aboard (chap. 7, 174), feeds off of Babbie.
58: Wind picks up before noon (186), and they sight island before sundown (187).
59: Next day, hiking the island, Horn and Seawrack talk of making a home there after bringing Silk to New Viron (188–89). They discover ruins of Vanished People (chap. 8, 191–92). Horn falls into pit, becomes unconscious (chap. 9, 196).
~: Horn sleeps for at least three days (196).
62: Night of no sleep.
63: In the morning Krait finds him (197), leaves.

64: The day Horn licks the dew and is visited by a Vanished Person who gives him a ghostly visit with Nettle (203).
65: Late afternoon, Krait visits a second time (203). They bargain, then Krait helps him escape (210). They meet Babbie. At night they reach the sloop (218).
66: Foggy morning. Krait arrives, guides them to Seawrack who is singing (chap. 10, 228). She is skittish, and Krait urges Horn to hold her and make her sing (231). She sings a few notes and he rapes her. That night they spot fires on the shore (242). Seawrack goes into the water (251).
67: Horn waits around all day and at sundown Seawrack drives a fish onboard. She gives him the Neighbor ring (253).
68: They make landfall on the western continent at the Land of Fires. At noon they reach the little river (V, chap. 11, 259), but it is near dark when they meet He-pen-sheep and family (261). He-pen-sheep tells Horn of a big river to the north (281). At night Horn goes out to meet Neighbors (263–64; 266–72) and meets Horn the Neighbor (273). On the way back he kills a breakbull (273).
69: Back on sloop (276). Horn must cut anchor line at night to avoid being dragged under (279), all because Krait had gone off hunting during his watch.
70: They see He-pen-sheep again, who gives them the head of the breakbull (280).
~:
~: Fish strip the flesh from the breakbull head in a few days (chap. 12, 292).
~:
~: They find the mouth of the river (293).
~:
~: Three days sailing up the river (293).
~: First day at Wichote (293). Probably the day Horn meets Yskin (296).
~: Second day at Wichote. Probably the day Horn and Seawrack try to enlist the shaman who brags of having put an invisible devil upon the trail of others (V, chap. 5, 137).
~: Third day at Wichote. Day after shaman episode, on the riverbank with Seawrack, Horn feels there are three of them, but it turns out he is counting Babbie (137).
~: Market day, and that night Krait says he found Pajarocu, ten days away (323).

~:
~: First week (323)
~: Meet Sinew coming down from Pajarocu (329).
~:
~: Presumably 3 days later they arrive in Pajarocu. During the day a few men show Horn and group the lander (351). At night, Seawrack senses night hunters, and Horn recognizes one of the men who had shown the lander visiting a nearby boat. He sees this man subdue the foreign woman there but does not understand it as such.
~: Market day. Horn figures out the lander is from Green (352). There is a meeting that night at the tavern Bush about the foreign woman who was bitten (353).
~: Horn and Sinew spread the word about the lander (359). That night Sinew and Horn plan method to leave Seawrack downstream.
~: The lander leaves with Horn, Sinew, and Krait (360–61). Trip probably takes weeks.
~:
~: Krait tries to divert lander to Long Sun Whorl but cannot (374).
~:
~: Krait visits Horn and tells him he has sabotaged one of the two inhumi needlers (373).
~:
~: Last fight on lander, Krait and inhumi barricaded in nose, Horn and group break in but are too late anyway (380).

Timeline for Gaon

Day: Note
~: Oreb flies off for over a year, or "the better part of a year" having the adventure of "The Night Chough" among others. Nine months (270 days) seems most likely.
~:
1: The Rajan begins writing (V, chap. 1, 18).
2: Second day of writing (18).
3: Writing about the day or two before Horn left Lizard (19).
4: The Rajan formalizes court of Gaon (25).
~:
8: Three days without writing (33).

9: Evening of above day or next day—three asterisk break (34).
10: Writing about decision not to return with the five (39).
11: Writing personal notes to his family (40).
12: Two farmers quarrel over a strip of land (41).
13: Writing of how long it has been since Horn left Lizard with regard to his sons, the Rajan writes, "Between birth and twenty, a year is an eternity" (46). Suggests it has been one year.
14: To do nothing is a talent (V, chap. 2, 49).
15: The Rajan puts paint on one lens of his glasses, presumably to hide his lost eye (54).
16: Writing about talking to Remora about gods (56).
17: Writing about prayer on sloop (58).
~:
21: A few days later (here four), the Rajan takes a day off and writes (66).
22: Writing about Marrow (69).
23: Writing about the robbery (74).
24: Writing about sailing to Mucor's Rock (77).
~:
27: Three days since he last wrote (78). Very late (93).
28: Writing the Tale of Pajarocu (V, chap. 5, 95).
29: Green bigger than a man's thumb last night (106). [Possibly late July, i.e., one year before conjunction?]
30: Inhuma caught last night (108).
31: Writing about Wijzer (123).
32: Writing about the accusation that *The Book of the Long Sun* is fiction (124).
~:
35: Not touched for three days, very late—near midnight (125). Storms have nearly wiped out the date palms.
36: Writing about the Thing on the Green Plain (126).
37: A visitor gives the Rajan a book on herbs called *The Healing Beds* (129).
38: Perhaps the next day, "In my last session" (131).
39: Mention of a shaman Horn and Seawrack met (137).
40: Writing about arriving at the Green Plain (140).
41: Elephant sacrifice (145).
42: Ambassadors from Skany (V, chap. 6, 147).
43: Writing about meeting Seawrack (156).
~: The Rajan goes to Skany and stays "most of the

summer" (158), which sounds like a period of 60 to 80 days. During this time an inhumu or inhuma is burned at Skany (V, chap. 10, 241).

103: Estimate 60 days in "A long while since" (158).
104: Writing about the second day with Seawrack (159).
105: Writing about meeting Captain Strik (167).
~:
107: Two days have passed (169).
108: Writing about leaving Strik's ship (V, chap. 7, 171).
109: Writing about meeting Krait on the sloop (173).
110: Writing about inhumi in general (183).
111: Writing about the rest of the night after Krait left the sloop (184).
112: Writing about sailing to the island of the pit (186).
113: Writing about hiking on the island (187).
114: Writing about falling into the pit (V, chap. 8, 191).
115: Writing about meeting Krait in the pit (chap. 9, 195).
116: Writing about negotiations with Krait and rescue (202).
117: A fortune-teller at court a few days ago (211).
118: Barsat comes to court to ask protection from the Vanished People (212).
119: Writing about going back to the sloop (213).
120: The Rajan goes hunting (215).
121: Writing prologue for a tangent on cattle (216). Weather sultry for at least a week (221).
122: The Rajan dreamt that Oreb was back (223).
123: The Rajan goes hunting again (chap. 10, 225).
124: Writing about the semi-feral Seawrack (227).
~:
131: A week later—a week of heat and terrible, violent storms (233). The Rajan writes of "The account I began last year" (234).
132: Writing about when Seawrack sang (234).
133: Writing about the day after (239).
134: The Rajan buries an inhumu and two inhuma (240).
~:
136: Writing about trying to return to normal (241).
~:
~: The big storm (245), the climax of conjunction. This should be about two years after Horn left Lizard.
~:

~: August 2nd—conjunction is past (246).
~: August 3rd—rain all day (251).
~: August 4th—writing about the Land of Fires (V, chap. 11, 255).
~: August 5th—writing about meeting He-pen-sheep (260).
~: August 6th—writing about bedding down at camp (263).
~: August 7th—Barsat and the Vanished People's house event (265). A Neighbor (Windcloud) gives the Rajan an ancient chalice.
~: August 8th—writing about meeting the Neighbors (266).
~: August 9th—writing about the hike back to camp (273).
~: August 10th—writing about sailing again (277).
~:
~: The War break (V, chap. 12, 283). Weeks or months later. The Rajan has been wounded (283) while upriver (299). He is suicidal (284).
~: The Rajan's forces pushed back again, nearly to town (287). The Rajan visits the front with Evensong, who interprets as he questions fresh prisoners on top of the elephant (288).
~: The Rajan sends Bahar and Namak downriver, Bahar to buy food, and Namak to hire mercenaries (290). The front is now an hour's ride away (291).
~: Four prisoners kill themselves (291).
~: The Rajan talks to prisoners (292).
~: The Rajan writes it is nearly two years since Horn found the river to Pajarocu (293), which was in Fall. Truce agreed to between Gaon and Han.
~: Hanese forces driven back (293).
~: Armorer visits in morning (298), the Rajan has secret mission for next day.
~: The Rajan rides elephant through impassable brush (299). Three boatloads of food from Bahar arrive (303).
~: Pounding rain (302). The rainy season has started (303). Winter wheat should have been planted (303).
~:
~: The Rajan returns after two days of rain—nearly 8 pm (304). They unearth Jahlee (V, chap. 13, 313).
~: The Rajan writes the next day about unearthing Jahlee (313).
~:
~: Four days after unearthing Jahlee, three days after last writing (322).

~: The Rajan in bed much of day (336).
~:
~: Away a long while. In another week the rainy season should end (V, chap. 14, 343). Oreb returns (346) after more than a year (369). [Implies he left before the rainy season the year before.]
~: Two a.m. escape (V, chap. 14, 355). The Rajan and Evensong in escape boat, heading down river (V, chap. 15, 363). Scylsday (365). They travel about one day down the river before stopping.
~: The war is over, won for Gaon, and so the inhumi are searching for the Rajan (V, chap. 16, 371). The Rajan leaves river, abandoning Evensong (376), trying to go northwest (377).
~:
~: Last time the Rajan ate was two days before (377). He meets a forest god (378).
~:
~: The Rajan meets Brother and Sister (378).
~: Second day with Brother and Sister.
~: Third day with Brother and Sister.
~: Fourth day with Brother and Sister.
~: The Rajan leaves Brother and Sister, they follow (379).
~: In morning, Brother and Sister are gone (379). At night the Rajan dreams of Pig and Hound (379).
~: The Rajan reads most of manuscript (380).

The total time the Rajan is in Gaon seems to be about a year. Oreb seems to have left shortly before the Rajan started writing, but the writing might have begun not on the first day in Gaon but after three months. The longer Oreb lingers, the more feathers he drops.

•

Appendix S1A2: Planet Blue as the Promised Land

Having discussed how *The Book of the Long Sun* has a layer of Moses and the Exodus out of Egypt, one supposes that *The Book of the Short Sun* will be somewhat analogous to the Israelites in Canaan, the Promised Land. The first post-Moses book of the Bible is Joshua, but this does not seem a good fit for planet Blue, since Horn does not seem to be modeled on the hero Joshua. After the Book of Joshua comes the Book of Judges, which seems appropriate as it describes a troubled situation, summed up in this key quote, "In those days there was no king in Israel: every man did that which was right in his own eyes" (Judges 21: 25).

Canaan had been divided up into twelve regions, one for each Israelite tribe, but during the time of the Judges, each territory went through a repeating cycle of rebellion and redemption. These waves of chaos, violence, murder, and mayhem match the hard times seen in "The Night Chough."

But something else, a ray of hope, emerges in *On Blue's Waters,* in the form of a wide-spread desire among the colonists for an anointed king in Caldé Silk, which translates to 1 Samuel, where the people demand a holy king to get them past the chaos of the Judges. In the Bible, this is a tricky request, as the Prophet Samuel tells them that any human king will be fallible, but the Israelites insist, thoroughly sick of the cycles of violence across nearly three hundred years.

So Horn is a bit like Samuel in that he is going forth to select this "good king" that the colonists have in mind, but then Wolfe fast-forwards the Bible into 2 Samuel, with the story of David. David is famous for killing Goliath as a young man, then for the sin of his relations with Bathsheba, followed by the tragic relationship with his son, Absalom. Horn starts to show similarities to David: his adulterous relationship with Seawrack, his complex relationship with the increasingly similar Sinew and Krait. Wolfe continues to race ahead, since Horn in Gaon has details that match King Solomon, the son of King David. The fact that Horn in Gaon is the one who starts writing finds a parallel to Solomon's penning three books in the Bible (Proverbs, Ecclesiastes, and Song of Songs). Solomon had many foreign wives, a situation that lured him away from monotheism.

When the Israelites took Canaan, they conquered the Philistine people, but the Philistine gods continued to lure the

Israelites into worshipping them. On Blue, the colonists do not displace a people, since the Neighbors have left the planet for some other place, and they graciously gift it to Horn as representative of humanity. Still, the gods of the Neighbors remain, and they seem to be active in luring the colonists into worshipping them. Then there are the inhumi, the devils of the Neighbors. The gods are probably the more benign of the Philistine gods, whereas the inhumi are the more malignant of the Philistine gods.

IN GREEN'S JUNGLES

(Volume VI)

Edition cited: Tor (hb), ISBN 978-0-3128-7315-8, 2000, 384 pp.

Dedication: "Respectfully dedicated to Maddie and Becca."
　Commentary: Wolfe's daughter Madeleine and her daughter. An earlier work dedicated to Becca is "The Old Woman Whose Rolling Pin is the Sun" (1991).

[Preface] 27th day of the Mobilization (13)

A letter during wartime from "Inclito" to "Incanto" about a failing war effort.
　Observation: The gist of the letter seems to be a commander telling a near equal that the military situation is hopeless and that he should make of show of force, then call a truce, and take the terms offered.

1. A New Beginning (15–34)

(Horn has paper again. While he is writing, a man named Inclito sits beside him and talks. Inclito invites him to dinner at his house away from town.)
　On Green, in the City of the Inhumi, Horn is awake in a cell where Sinew and the others are sleeping. A Neighbor comes along with a job for him, to clear a clogged sewer, by himself.

They walk a number of blocks and the Neighbor anoints his face with a sweet-smelling oil.

(Horn speaks with the stationer, Atteno.)

The Neighbor offers Horn a selection of swords. Horn asks him to make the selection. It is the black sword.

* * *

(Inclito picked up Horn at the stationer's shop. On the ride to his house, Inclito explains that the towns nearby were all seeded from one city on the Long Sun Whorl, and now they are fighting each other. This town is Blanko, a democracy. In Soldo they have a duko.)

(Inclito asks if Horn knows Silk. Horn says he knew him once. Inclito says he will not ask his name. Horn asks him to suggest one. Inclito gives "Incanto," after his elder brother who died in infancy. Inclito says he has a spy in his house.)

Unusual Terms and Phrases

Corpo—Italian "body," in this case, the legislative body of Blanko.

Observation: Where the war in Gaon was foreign invasion (Chinese versus Hindu), the situation at Blanko is fighting among Italophones. As such it suggests a link to the Italian unification (1848–1871). Perhaps Inclito bears some resemblance to Mazzini and/or Garibaldi.

Italophone: The words "Blanko" and "Duko" are not Italian: they are Esperanto. The use of "K" is a giveaway.

Spaghetti Western: Italian cinema, "the man with no name," with its root in Japanese samurai movies (e.g., Kurosawa's *Yojimbo* [1961]) which are in turn secretly derived from American hardboiled detective fiction (e.g., Hammett's *Red Harvest* [1929]).

Long Sun Whorl hints: Pig wore a rag over his eyes (18–19).

2. Stories before Dinner (35–49)

(Horn, sleeping in a barrel behind the shop, is visited by a woman wearing perfume. But he turns to writing about the dinner.)

(There is the grandmother, her granddaughter Mora, Mora's friend Fava, and Inclito. They regularly play a story-telling game, and they do so now.)

(Fava tells "The Washed Child," her own experience where she met a dirty woman washing a child in a mountain stream. The woman admitted she planned to drown the boy. Fava rescued him, but then they all ended up in court. The judge ruled in Fava's favor, and she started back home with the boy, but he vanished the second night. A year later she visited and heard from neighborhood children that the boy had been taken by the Vanished People.)

(Mora tells "The Giant's Daughter," a fable about ugly Mora and pretty Fava.)

(Inclito tells "The Sentry and His Brother," a true crime mystery involving two brothers who hated each other.)

Unusual Terms and Phrases

Dervis—Italian "dervish," a wandering holy man.

Sleeps in a Barrel: Diogenes the Cynic, or Huckleberry Finn. John William Waterhouse's painting *Diogenes* (1882) has the philosopher in his barrel with a scroll across his knee, being visited by three young women in fashionable attire. This sounds remarkably close to Horn being visited by a mysterious woman at his barrel.

3. The Mother's Reminiscence: From the Grave (50–59)

(The grandmother tells an episode of her life in the Long Sun Whorl. As a young woman she was courted by two men, Turco and Casco. She favored Turco. War came. Casco was violently jealous, threatening violence. She visited him in the hospital on her wedding day but he was unconscious. He visited her in her mourning over her husband Turco, as they had married at that hospital bed and she brought him home to die. Casco went to the grave, came back, and died within minutes. A servant spied on him at the grave and saw a tall man with a bird on his shoulder, both man and bird speaking to Casco before vanishing like ghosts. Casco then desecrated the grave.)

(She married again the next summer. He fell over dead on a hunting trip in autumn.)

(Three years later she married a third time. About seventeen months later he died doing ditch work on a farm.)

(Then she married a different type of man, and they had children, the first son who died, and then Inclito. The husband found the old boot with a viper fang in it; the poison killed Casco, then the subsequent husbands.)

(Before telling the story he told, Horn writes about a dream he had after dinner: he was back in the pit, reading a copy of the Chrasmologic Writings in which an illustration of Scylla struggled to get out of the page. Horn awoke in the shop with Oreb saying, "Watch out!")

Observation: Part of what makes the story so strange is that the strego the grandmother encountered as a teen seems so much like Silk and Oreb, yet the strego appeared long before Silk met Oreb. That is the sense of it, and the numbers to back it up require some guessing: figure that this family came to Blue 13 years ago (after Mora was born, and she is in her "early teens"); guess that Inclito was 20 at that time (adding the years since Salica's successful fourth marriage); and add an additional seven years to the date when the strego appeared, for a grand total of 40 years ago. Silk was around five years old then. This accounting would mean that Salica is 53 years old, which might seem young for "elderly."

4. My Own Story: The Man with the Black Sword (60–73)

(Horn tells of a man with a sword led by phantom-like Vanished People through the City of Inhumi. They go down to the entrance of the sewer, and the man prays at the altar of a Vanished Goddess of purity. The altar gives him a magic light. He continues deeper in.)

(He comes upon a blind man who is eating corpses, a survivor who had been cast away as dead by the inhumi. The blind man does not remember his name or the city of the Long Sun Whorl he came from; the man suggests he might be Auk.)

(The blind man takes him to the logjam of corpses. The swordsman works to clear them out. When the blind man tries to kill him, the dam gives way, washing him out of the city, ending the story.)

(The party talk about topics raised by the stories. Horn realizes Fava is an inhuma.)

Observation: Horn continues the story he began writing in chapter 1. This re-framing, or continuing the tale in a different context, seems akin to narrative tricks in the Arabian Nights.

Myth: Clearing the sewer is a lot like a labor of Heracles, specifically the cleaning of the Augean Stables. Heracles cleaned the filthy stables by rerouting the rivers Alpheus and Peneus. This was labor number five out of twelve.

Note: The blind man in the sewers (64) in contrast to the note before (V, chap. 3), but the blind man claims he is not blind (65).

Long Sun Whorl hints: Hyacinth's ghost and its effect upon Pig (70).

5. In Green's Jungle (74–100)

(The next night, Horn writes late after sleeping in the barrel through the afternoon. He has received two letters.)

* * *

(Fava's letter is mentioned, then how it was Mora who visited at the barrel. He confronts her about Fava being an inhuma and she admits it is true. They talk about Fava's story about the Washed Child and Horn asks Mora for the real ending. She weeps but denies, saying that Fava made it up. Horn says they both know Fava is slowly killing her grandmother.)

(Horn attributes the Outsider as sending the leatherskin to

prove that being alone is not the worst evil.)

On Green, Krait is dying in the jungle, and Horn offers his arm for feeding. Krait refuses. Then Krait tells him the secret and dies.

* * *

(Now it is morning. Horn starts writing again. He gives the text of Inclito's letter, then that of Fava's. He gives more of the conversation with Mora. He tells her about Scleroderma, who surprised everyone with her bravery.)

* * *

On Green, Horn is searching for the sword and the light, ignoring all the corpses that haunt him still.

(Horn detects that Onorifica the kitchen maid is trysting with someone. He thinks it is Inclito. Fava and Mora enter the room.)

The Blanko Hanky-Panky: While looking for the spy, Horn notices that the kitchen maid Onorifica has been trysting (93). "The other maid is slender and more attractive" (93). Onorifica has been given a silver ring (94). Torda is the other maid (94). Onorifica says of Torda and Inclito, "Only they was always fighting. That was how it was when I came" (94).

Sleeps in a Barrel: It is interesting that the mystery of Horn's visitor ends up having three suspects, the first being a woman, the second being the "girl" Fava, the third being the girl Mora.

Long Sun Whorl hints: "[A]musing them with stories of my journey to Viron with Pig and Hound" (96).

6. The Guessing Game (101–109)

On Green, Horn avoids going back to the cell, tries to get away from the City. He finds the alien light, and reasons that it floated far, where the sword must have sunk immediately, so he turns and goes back to the City. It is a day later when he locates the sword and it comes to his hand.

(Riding in the coach with Fava and Mora, Fava gets them to play "the guessing game.")

The Blanko Hanky-Panky: Horn notes, "[W]e were admitted by the sullen chambermaid" (109).

7. Second Stories (110–19)

(They play the storytelling game again at dinner.)

(Salica's second story: Stuck in the Chimney. A trader frightens a witch that her husband has fallen down the chimney. She sees to it that his fat wife is pulled up into a chimney to her death.)

(Mora's second story: The False Friend and the True Friend. The story of a good girl and a bad girl, where the twist is that the bad girl's name is 'Mora.')

(Inclito's second story: The Mercenary's Employer. The experience of a merc who is looking for work after winning the war for Gaon.)

8. My Second Story: The Man Who Returned (120–27)

The leader returns to the City. He fails to convince the hundred men that they should find and take the lander. Instead, they vote to find women on Green, so he leads them forth, looking for another lander among colony sites. After some losses, he gives them his ultimatum of going back to the City.

(Horn pauses his telling as he hears "Hyacinth singing to her waves.")

The leader slips away in the night, before the vote in the morning. Over the days, others join him.

(Oreb interrupts.)

They fight their way to the landing pad, but the lander is gone. As they fight their way out, they are joined by a stranger. The leader is wounded and the stranger is wounded. When the stranger can no longer walk, the leader stays behind with him.

(Salica says Horn can stop the telling, but he presses on.)

The stranger reveals he is Krait, the leader's inhumu son.

(The listeners react.)

Krait gives him the secret. The leader rejoins the men. After a time, they find a ruined lander. They begin to repair it. But then the leader's human son finds a woman in one of the settlements and turns against his father for good.

One by one the remaining men die. Then the last two leave him to die alone.

(The listeners give him handkerchiefs.)

The leader raises the ring to his eye. A Neighbor comes and aids him with a miracle, sending his spirit into the body of a person whose spirit is dying.

(That is where Horn ends the story being spoken, but Horn writes that he found himself transported to the Long Sun Whorl, beside a dead woman in her coffin.)

Edgar Rice Burroughs: This action on Green recalls not Barsoom but Pellucidar, the prehistoric hollow Earth, dominated by the flying reptile-men the Mahars, beginning with *At the Earth's Core* (1914).

Bible: This part fills in that missing "Joshua" side of things. Here the inhumi are the Philistines.

History: This episode has a "Spartacus" feel to it. In the Third Servile War of the Roman Republic, a group of gladiators led by Spartacus broke free to loot, pillage, and grow in number. Starting in Capua by Naples, the rebels followed a gyrating path. By 71 BC the group of 2,000 men were in the south near the Strait of Messina, where pirates hired to transport them to Sicily took the money but abandoned them. The rebels then moved away from the toe of the boot to the heel of the boot, where they were finally wiped out.

Seawrack Singing Now: Only he calls her "Hyacinth" (121).

Observation: Transition from story in third person (120–21) to first person (121–22), back to third (122–27).

Long Sun Whorl hints: Horn writes about how he found himself on the Long Sun Whorl beside a coffin containing a middle-aged woman (127).

9. Fava's Second Story: The Girl on Green (128–47)

(A girl hatches on Green. She swims with other babies in the river. She sees Horn's leader character and follows him. The leader saves her and tells her how to grow rapidly. He wants her help in thwarting his son.)

***

(The narrative jumps back to a thread begun in Chapter 5, where nightgowned Fava and Mora want to talk with Horn, but instead he talks to the sullen maid Torda, saying she is the spy. He outlines how she began an affair with Inclito, but something went wrong. Mora sends Fava on a task, then confesses she is the spy, having cracked under the pressure of Horn's ploy. Fava was the first spy, and she recruited Mora.)

(As Horn discusses things with Fava, reality begins to warp and the four of them seem to be on Green. Fava talks with Salica's memories. Mucor enters the scene to report to both Silk and Horn. The cook enters to announce breakfast.)

The Blanko Hanky-Panky: Horn finally gets to talk with Torda, and he lowers the boom: "Inclito . . . treated you as well as his daughter. All four of us know why" (135). He later says Inclito "doesn't want to remarry" (136). Torda admits she is from Novella Citta (136). Horn declares, "Torda was clearly a rejected lover" (137). He refrains from detailing how Inclito had pivoted from Torda to trysting with Onorifica.

Secret Cupid: Horn then instructs Fava, "Tell Duko Rigoglio that Inclito is about to marry a woman from Novella Citta, and that both Novella Citta and Olmo have agreed to support his counterattack on Soldo once the war has begun" (145).

Observation: Fava's story uses character from Horn's story.

Note: Babbie returned to Mucor without Horn, so she began searching and here has found Silk and Horn (146–47).

10. Untamed Talents (148–70)

(Horn, Mora, and Oreb go in to breakfast.)

(Horn jumps ahead to dinner and the two young men assigned to carry messages from Horn to Novella Citta and Olmo. They talk over the message from the sacrifice, that enemy armies are on the move, and only one of the two messengers would set out in the morning.)

(After dinner, Mora interrupts his writing. She asks about the news of a son seeking his father, a man whose description does not sound like Horn. She asks him about the warpage that made it seem they were on Green, and did Horn really try to use an inhuma to fool his son?)

In talking with Mora, Horn mentally goes back to Green at that time when Krait is dying.

(Mora's words bring him back. He tells her that Silk had been a frozen embryo whose special talent was leadership. Horn tells of the personal hardship he had experienced because Silk did not come to Blue.)

(Then he talks with Inclito about battle plans.)

Secret Cupid: Presumably the letters to be delivered by Eco and Rimando (chapter 10, 148) contain the same information that Horn gave Fava about Inclito's imminent marriage to a woman from Novella Citta, and that both Novella Citta and Olmo have agreed to support Inclito's counterattack on Soldo once the war has begun.

11. In the Field (171–82)

(Horn writes from a military camp, two days later.)

(Back to the narrative: The next morning they find that Mora had gone, taking Rimando's horse and message. Eco rides off after her. Inclito rides off after her. Horn talks Rimando down and makes some order in the chaos.)

(Horn talks with a patrol that spotted the enemy in a saddle on the nearby hill. He goes with them and uses his "bush-walking" skill. He sends his men back to camp and goes on with Oreb to the enemy camp, where he recognizes a number of mercenaries he had hired at Gaon. He talks with them and learns they captured Inclito and Mora. Horn talks them into switching sides.)

Plutarch: There is something about mercs switching sides in this manner that sounds like a detail from Plutarch.

12. An Exchange of Prisoners (183–91)

(Another two days later, Horn writes how it went.)

(At the prisoner exchange, Horn conceals his surprise that the "daughter" is Fava. Horn tells Inclito how he raised the troop at Blanko and marched forth.)

(But the crowd nearly turns on itself. Horn offers to exchange himself for Inclito and Fava. They trade him for Inclito alone.)

13. Escape to Green (192–207)

(Horn writing from back in Blanko. He tells:)

(He and Fava huddle in a bush in the cold night, guarded by four troopers. They warp to a hot cell on Green. Human slaves come in, and the big one knocks down a trooper. An inhumu master leaps upon the downed man, and the big slave sounds like Auk when he tells them to escape. Another trooper shoots the master dead and the slaves grab the body and go.)

(Horn believes he is dreaming. He turns his mind to the problem of convincing the mercs to join the Blanko side. His two military tricks, sending Fava one way and the two messages meant to be intercepted, have apparently failed.)

(Fava talks with him and they discover she is a real girl here. Horn talks with the troopers, asks for his staff. They look but they do not have it. Horn concentrates on Oreb and Oreb appears, in a strange form. He concentrates on the black sword and it materializes in his hand.)

14. Duko Rigoglio (208–23)

(Horn taps flagstones, willing one to sound hollow. They find one and lift it to expose a stairway. Fava, Oreb, and Horn take the stairs, leaving the mercs behind, but there is another merc in the sewers, a trooper who had come to check on them in the snow. Actually, he is a Blanko trooper sent by Inclito.)

(As they move through the dangerous sewer, Horn develops a theory about this weird space-warping power. He asks Fava to concentrate on a room she has visited in the Duko's palace in Soldo. She does so, and they warp there.)

(They meet with the Duko. It turns out he was a sleeper on the Long Sun Whorl, and he speaks of Nessus. After a while, the mercs from the sewer catch up and one fires at the Duko.)

* * *

(Horn shifts the timeframe to his current problem of raising money at Blanko. The difficulty of dealing with men who only want to cheat the mercs. How Horn raised a militia of boys, old men, and women; then how he jailed the leaders of those who jeered.)

Barsoom: The space-warping talent recalls that of John Carter. In *A Princess of Mars* (1912), John Carter is transported willy-nilly from Earth to the other planet, arriving without external materials, not even clothing, but by the fifth novel, *Chessmen of Mars* (1922), he has learned how to actively teleport himself with clothes and weapons.

15. Before the Battle (224–35)

(Horn writes as the town celebrates. The Duko has turned against Olmo, and Olmo asks Blanko for help. But Fava died on Green, while two troopers who died there are alive on Blue but scrambled so they cannot speak or understand spoken words.)

* * *

(On this night Sfido visits Horn. It has been ten days. Sfido asks to be hired for Blanko to lead the militia.)

16. A Young Man from the South (236–46)

(Horn has brought his mercs from Blue. His goal is to wipe out the inhumi of the City.)

(Back in Blanko, he hears rumor that Mora and Eco escaped from jail. On the bad side, Olmo has fallen. As for the coming invasion, Horn has a strategy of deception set around a farm north of Blanko.)

***

(Ditches dug.)

***

(Last of big guns arrive and are hidden.)

***

(Walls completed.)

***

(Inclito leads fighting retreat.)

Unusual Terms and Phrases

Cuoio—Italian "leather."

Solaria—sunrooms.

Unintended Consequences: As a result of the deceptive report and letters, former allies looted and burned Olmo.

Preface Delivery: The letter given in the preface is delivered to Horn. Reading it here, it seems to be a smoking gun regarding Inclito's trysting with Onorifica, and his preference for Torda.

Observation: Sfido has not yet read the letter from Inclito to Incanto (239), but his assessment of the coming battle situation (240–41) is the same.

Seawrack Singing Now: (246).

17. The Battle of Blanko (247–69)

(The old woman of the farmhouse is Jahlee.)

(Telling about the battle, first the enemy officer demands surrender. Horn refuses.)

(The attack comes, led by cavalry coming through the winter wheat. They encounter trip cords and boars tethered with long ropes. Followed by fireworks. And then the hidden artillery.)

(At a lull, Horn takes up a truce flag and walks forward. He

talks a bit again with Colonel Terzo, until the latter flees.)
***

(After the battle, a representative from Novella Citta arrives. He has word on Mora, and his horde is coming soon.)

Unusual Terms and Phrases

Peel house—a small, fortified keep or tower house.

Observation: Horn took Inclito's letter to heart, that his ragtag volunteers would only "fight from behind walls," and built them walls of sandbags in the farmland (255–56).

Seawrack Singing Now: Heard by another.

Song: The Siren's song begins, "In our small house with shining windows . . ." (267).

> *In our small house with shining windows,*
> *I waited till the tide brought your wreck through.*
> *Lie here beside me in the darkness.*
> *I'll wake to life the corpse I say is you.*

This poem might be original to Wolfe. It is a woman's answer to the man's song "Sad Experience Teaches Me" (V, chap. 16). Coming from Seawrack, it is especially chilling since she was so "cute."

Secret Cupid: The representative from Novella Citta asks Horn, "Duko Inclito is marrying a woman from Novella Citta?" (268)

18. The End and Afterward (270–80)

(Back to the battle: after the truce talk, a desperate second attack that fades after three waves.)

(During the night, the Soldese try a sneak attack, using the Ducal Bodyguard, less than one hundred.)
***

(The day after the battle, Horn solves the problems in a masterful way. Then, after a few days of pursuit, he captures the

Duko, General Morello, and Colonel Terzo.)

(Horn, after talking with the Duko, realizes he was a sleeper back in the Long Sun Whorl. Rigoglio says the name "Roger" was printed on his sleeping tube. Mucor appears in the smoke and says she will send Babbie.)

Unusual Terms and Phrases
Chain (distance)—a unit of length equal to 66 feet.

19. Say Father (281–96)

(Oreb finds a sacrifice table in the hills. Horn travels there and finds a wonderous white table. He plans an experiment to warp to Green again.)

(Lacking an animal to sacrifice, he offers instead a piece of bread and some wine, following a pattern he recently saw on the Long Sun Whorl.)

(The Outsider comes to stand behind him.)

(In the presence of the Outsider, Horn is conscious of another world, a place all around but not seen.)

(While he is communing with the god, a baletiger walks around the horse a few times, then leaves.)

(Horn reports how his son Hide is part of the group fighting for Blanko. In the dark Horn leads Hide to the baletiger and beyond it to the grave of Fava. The baletiger drives game to them so they can kill and make sacrifice.)

Bible: The humble sacrifice of bread and wine links directly to the communion instituted by Jesus among his disciples at the Last Supper:

> *And he took bread, and gave thanks, and brake it, and gave unto them, saying, This is my body which is given for you: this do in remembrance of me.*
>
> *Likewise also the cup of wine after supper, saying, This cup is the new testament in my blood, which is shed for you.* (Luke 22: 19–20)

Observation: This is the second time Horn feels the presence of the Outsider at a sacrifice, the other time being during the fish sacrifice at Mucor's Rock (V, chap. 3).

Plato's Cave: Continuing his growth of understanding, Horn writes,

> In the presence of the Outsider, I was conscious of another whorl. Not a remote one like Green or the Long Sun Whorl . . . but a whorl that is as present to us as this one, a place all around us that we cannot see into. Many would say that it is not real, but that is almost the reverse of truth. It is the things of this whorl that are unreal by standards of that one. (VI, chap. 19, 285)

This seems to form a basic feeling for the colonists, that they are getting away from the false or at least capricious gods of the Long Sun Whorl and going to an empty place where they can be free.

Long Sun Whorl hints: Horn had no knife when he sacrificed for Olivine (284).

Observation: "Perhaps the god-spell hasn't worn off yet" (292), regarding the protection against the baletiger.

20. Back at the Battlefield (297–311)

(At the farmhouse, Horn is sick.)

* * *

(Horn begins his experiment to visit Sinew on Green. Then Mora and Eco arrive. Mora tells Horn about her experience and marriage. Then Horn selects the participants. He gives a speech that sounds like a farewell. Then they warp.)

Observation: Horn says, "I've been talking with a goddess in my own dreams almost every time I sleep" (305).

21. The Red Sun (312–21)

(They arrive at the Red Sun Whorl, to a city Rigoglio identifies as Nessus. Rigoglio is attacked and wounded. Horn admits he was trying to transport them to Green, to show them "what real evil is" [321].)

Observation: The Red Sun is so large that Horn's outstretched hand could not cover it (313).

The fact that Rigoglio inadvertently hijacked the warp implies he has the greater power in this instance, due to his greater will (as a sleeper) or deeper despair (as a captured leader).

Unusual Terms and Phrases
Omophagist—an eater of raw flesh.

22. The Barbican and the Bear Tower (322–37)

(After returning to Blue, Horn talks with Jahlee and Hide. They talk about the Red Sun Whorl.)

(Horn returns to his narrative. They meet a fantastically dressed man by the river and talk with him as they walk through the vast ruins.)

* * *

(Horn and Hide are traveling together on Blue. They talk about Horn's book in progress.)

* * *

(Horn and Hide have to go around a marsh. That night they talk again about the book in progress.)

(Horn picks up at the Red Sun Whorl where they had arrived at the cemetery gate and talked with the guard there.)

(Horn returns to his camp on Blue. He has a father/son talk with Hide.)

(Horn picks up the Red Sun Whorl thread, how the guard marched them around to the barbican. The lochage writes them a pass to the bear tower.)

Unusual Terms and Phrases

Barbican—an outer fortification or defense to a city or castle, especially a double tower erected over a gate or bridge; often made strong and lofty and serving as a watchtower.

Lochage—[LOCK-ij] leader of a "lochus," a 100-man unit of the army in Sparta and some other Greek states.

23. Why Are the Inhumi Like Us? (338–55)

(Hide and Horn at the marsh are joined by Jahlee. Horn and Jahlee politely argue until she leaves. Then Horn tells how she had taken over the farmhouse after the owners had fled.)

(Hide asks about the Vanished People. In talking about them, Horn confesses he commanded more than twenty inhumi back in Gaon, using them as spies and assassins. They talk about the presumed history of the inhumi and the Vanished People.)

Bible: Wolfe describes the mundane physical impersonation where Jahlee passes herself off as an old farmwife by taking up residence in an abandoned house. This seems like a sly nod to the New Testament model of discussing spiritual possession in terms of invaders taking over a physical house, a model that Wolfe appears to be using with regard to possession in the Long Sun and Short Sun books. In the Gospel of Matthew, Jesus says directly:

> *Or else how can one enter into a strong man's house, and spoil his goods, except he first bind the strong man? and then he will spoil his house.* (Matthew 12: 29)

The "house" is the victim's body, and in this case the intruding spirit has first tied up the victim's spirit. Jesus gives another example later in Matthew:

> *When the unclean spirit is gone out of a man, he walketh through dry places, seeking rest, and findeth none. Then*

he saith, I will return into my house from whence I came out; and when he is come, he findeth it empty, swept, and garnished. Then goeth he, and taketh with himself seven other spirits more wicked than himself, and they enter in and dwell there: and the last state of that man is worse than the first. (Matthew 12: 43-45)

This time there is no talk of the owner; instead, there is an unclean spirit that was cast out to wander in the weird wastes, but since God was not installed to protect the place, the demon returned and brought some wicked friends.

24. Sinew's Village (356–74)

(Writing by campfire light, Horn warps to Green as he falls asleep. Jahlee, Oreb, and Hide are there. Hide has scouted ahead and found a village named Qarya. They visit this settlement, searching for Sinew. Maliki questions them, then leads them to await Sinew's return at his log house. They meet Sinew's wife Bala and her two sons. The guests admit they are ghosts or dreams. Bala admits the bad smell is from the prisoners downstairs. These prisoners are "inhumans," former slaves of the City of inhumi. Horn talks about old times with Maliki, who thinks he is Caldé Silk no matter what he says. Hide comes back up, disturbed by one of the prisoners, a woman.)

Unusual Terms and Phrases
   Maliki—a Turkish word meaning "owner."
   Miralaly—probably a typo for "miralay," a former Turkish rank of colonel, here used as a courtesy title.
   Qarya—Armenian term for village or town.
   Rais-man—"Rais" is Arabic word meaning "leader, chief." Presumably "-man" is added because in Trivigaunte a rais is always a woman.
   Observation: When Jahlee says, "Your father's twice the man you are," and Hide says, "I know" (358), he is probably looking

past the cliché, instead referring to the dual Horn/Silk nature. When Hide says the elder does not look like Horn (358), this suggests that the Silk side is currently dominant.

Curious Continuations: By bringing an inhuma to Sinew's village, Horn is following through on the story he began with Fava (VI, chap. 9), who built on his story (VI, chap. 4), itself a continuation of Horn's written narrative (VI, chap. 1).

25. The God of Blue (375–84)

(Jahlee had been away from Horn and Hide for two days when she arrives by the campfire at night. They discuss many things, including the inhuman prisoners Chenille and Auk, and the fact that Maliki's real name is Colonel Abanja.)

* * *

(In the morning, Hide asks if Jahlee had been there, because he had dreamed he was back on Green.)

(At night, Jahlee visits. After Hide falls asleep and Jahlee leaves, Vanished People visit Horn. They listen to him, but they will not answer his questions about their gods.)

* * *

(Nearly a week later, a time of constant rain and snow, which saw Horn and Hide camped in a cave.)

(Morning comes and they set out. Overtaking a regal lady on a white mule, they agree to travel together for her protection. At the inn near sunset they discover she is Jahlee, and Horn introduces her as his daughter.)

Unintended Consequences: As a result of Horn's second attack on the City of the inhumi, Auk and Chenille are compelled to capture others and, having failed, their five adopted children have been killed.

APPENDICES FOR IN GREEN'S JUNGLES

Appendix S2A1: Timelines for In Green's Jungles

Timeline from Green to the Long Sun Whorl

Day: Note
1: Horn and the other humans are in the underground prison. After Krait's brief visit, Horn gets the sewer job from a Neighbor (VI, chap. 1, 20).
2: Searching all day for the sword and light lost at the end of the sewer job (chap. 6, 101). At night he finds the light (102).
3: At night Horn finds the sword (103).
4: Horn goes back to free Sinew and the others (chap. 5, 91).
5: Perhaps the next day, Horn, unable to persuade the 100 men to retake the lander, agrees to lead them in search of colonists (chap. 8, 120). They go north.
~:
~: They fight a small settlement. There are 69 men left. Horn goes back to retake the lander and 45 men follow him. The hike back takes 4+ days.
~:
~: They fight their way to the landing spot, but the lander is gone. Down to 27 men (123). They fight inhumans, human slaves of the inhumi, and Horn is wounded.
~:
~: Krait, who had joined them, is wounded. The inhumans pursue them into the jungle.
~:
~: Krait and Horn left behind. Krait dies in jungle (V, chap. 16,

374; VI, chap. 5, 81; chap. 8, 124).
~:
~: Horn catches up with group.
~:
~: They travel far.
~:
~: They find deserted settlement with a ruined lander (125). They work at repairing the lander.
~:
~: Sinew finds a woman at one of the settlements they raid and turns against Horn (126).
~:
~: One by one Horn's men die.
~:
~: Horn is riding the three-horned beast when he is mortally wounded (V, chap. 3, 94).
~:
~: Fava goes to Soldo again and hears rumors of Bricco (VI, chap. 2, 43).
~:
~: As Horn is dying, his last two men leave, taking both the sword and the light. Horn uses the ring, and a female Neighbor takes his spirit to place in a body on the Long Sun Whorl. The body had belonged to Silk (VI, chap. 8, 127).

Timeline for Blanko

Day: Note
1: Horn in village of woodcutter Cugino (VI, chap. 1, 16), located one day south of Blanko (VI, chap. 2, 37). He has soup (VI, chap. 1, 24). A good woman fixes his torn robe (23).
2: Horn arrives in Blanko.
3: Horn starts writing, meets Inclito (VI, chap. 1). Nearly a week since he heard any news from Gaon (29). Agrees to take the name Incanto. Goes to dinner at Inclito's house. First storytelling game. Horn sleeps at the stationer's shop. Dreams of being back in pit (chap. 3, 58).
4: Horn spends most of daylight hours sleeping off the heavy meal in alley barrel (chap. 5, 74). A week or 10 days since leaving Evensong (75). In the morning he talks with Mora (76). She says Inclito will write a letter to him, and she

promises one when she gets home from palaestra (78). Middle of afternoon in barrel (chap. 2, 35). Horn gets letter from Inclito, urging him to come and stay at the house (83–84). Then there is a letter from Fava. He goes to the palaestra, gives coachman a note to Inclito saying he would come not that day but the next (96). Night at stationer's shop (chap. 5, 74). Midnight (75).

5: Morning (83). Afternoon ride with the girls Mora and Fava to house (chap. 6, 104). Night (93). Second storytelling game (110). First experience of warping to Green (chap. 9, 145; 156), a "dream" interrupted by the Cook (chap. 13, 194).

6: After midnight, a nightmare awakens him at Inclito's house and he writes about searching for sword on Green (chap. 5, 90). He questions the kitchen maid (93). He tries to sleep again, writes more. Maid brings tea and tarts (94). Writing about night of Day 5 (chap. 9, 133). Dawn. Fields about to be plowed for winter wheat (140). Breakfast. Sacrifice of a young bull reveals message from the Outsider and the Mother that the horde of Soldo has already set out to invade Blanko (chap. 10, 151). Dinner with two messengers (148).

7: In the morning, Mora rides off with message (chap. 11, 171). Inclito goes after her, and both are captured (181). Horn goes to Blanko, as ordered (chap. 12, 185). Horde (20 cavalry, 96 infantry) marches forth—first day of Mobilization (presumably). They nearly reach the last plowlands before they camp (186).

8: Second day of march halts at night on word that enemy is near, at saddle. Vivo arrives with additional troops, bringing the total to 250. At night in camp, Horn writes about morning of Day 7 (171). Then on patrol he meets mercenaries at saddle (180–82). He writes of this immediately after.

9: Horn trades himself for Inclito (chap. 12, 191). He is held with Fava, whom the mercenaries think is Mora (192). They huddle in the snow and warp to Green, taking along Captain Kupus's company of 200 men. Horn warps Oreb over, where he appears the size of a four-year-old child (chap. 13, 203). Horn offers to return them to Blue if they leave the service of Soldo. They refuse and he leaves them in the prison cell, going into the sewer.

10: After midnight Valico finds them there and says the whole camp is sleeping (chap. 14, 210). Horn has Fava think of Duko's palace in Soldo, and they warp there (215). Fava, Valico, Horn, and Oreb meet Duko and sue for peace. He refuses. The other mercenaries follow Oreb in and try to shoot the Duko but then they are back on Green (220). Kupus pledges to follow him (chap. 15, 226). They take Sfido's needler (230). They fight a worm in the sewer that kills Chaku and Teras (224). They fight against the City of Inhumi, intending to kill all inhumi (chap. 16, 236–38). When they warp back to Blue they find Chaku and Teras alive (224), but Fava has died in the snow.

11: Writing about Day 9 (chap. 12, 183). With Kupus's 200 and another group that arrives, Horn now has more than 300 fresh mercenaries.

~:

~: Horn returns to Blanko, stays with Atteno the stationer (chap. 13, 192). He writes more about Day 9. The tenth of the month is only three days distant (195). The citizens are raising money (chap. 14, 220), but they want to cheat the mercenaries (222).

~:

32: Blanko celebrating in evening at news that Olmo, besieged by Soldo, requests aid from Blanko. Horn is still at Atteno's, where he writes about Day 9 and the mercenaries in the sewer on Green (chap. 15, 224). Sfido arrives at door, first seen in ten days (227).

33: After midnight, Horn writes of Sfido's visit (226). During the day, Sfido and Horn drill Blanko troops.

34: Sfido and Horn drill Blanko troops (chap. 16, 238).

35: Horn writing of Days 33 to 34. Rimando arrives with letter (preface) from Inclito (238), dated 27th day of the Mobilization. [Which means Day 34+, if Mobilization starts on Day 7.] Olmo has fallen (238).

~: March two days to outpost location, where they dig ditches, sew thousands of sacks.

38: Preparations for battle (241–43). Colbacco brings new men from the south, including Cugino and a boy who looks like Hoof and Hide (244).

39: Morning—snowing (243). Horn at farmhouse. Dinner with the old woman (244).

40: Battle of Blanko. A few days after the letter (VI, chap. 17,

255). At this point the mercenaries had been with them almost half a month (253). Winter wheat is tall enough to hide a boar. Retreating Blanko troopers, 50 to 100, pass through after dawn (chap. 16, 244–45). Inclito is in the rearguard, which stays (245). The battle begins an hour or two past noon (258). Horn and Terzo parlay. Second attack comes 15 minutes later (chap. 18, 270). They have shattered the Dragoons (269). Horn forms up a group to give chase into the hills, in the morning (272). He writes about seeing a boy who looks like Hoof and Hide on Day 38.

41: Midnight, writing a bit about the battle of Blanko, promising to write more next day (chap. 16, 245). Old woman visits and Horn realizes she is Jahlee (248). After midnight, the second attack (VI, chap. 16, 246; chap. 18, 272) by the Ducal Bodyguard who forded the river (272–73). They wipe out the Bodyguard (269). Morning after battle (274). Horn takes a large force and moves to catch up with Inclito. Evening in the hills, not at the farmhouse (chap. 17, 247). Writing about the Battle of Blanko (248–67).

42: Catch up with Inclito on second day (chap. 18, 275). A representative from Novella Citta arrives with 450 troopers (chap. 17, 267).

43: Horn writes "The End and Afterward" (chap. 18, 270–73) about the battle. He hopes to find an altar the next day (274).

44: Horn writes about the morning of Day 41 (274), then reports that on the current day they discovered the Duko disguised among their prisoners (275). Horn interviews Duko Rigoglio, and Mucor appears in the campfire smoke to say that Babbie has returned (280).

45: Oreb finds an altar of the Vanished People on a hill to north (chap. 19, 281). Horn plans experiment to visit Green the next night (283). Horn meets Cuoio and sees he is Hide. They sit on Fava's gravestone (293). Hide says Horn left Lizard about three years ago (294). Baletiger episode, in which Cuoio kills game driven toward them. Horn becomes ill that night (chap. 20, 297). Horn writes about the day (chap. 19, 281).

46: Morning at Jahlee's farmhouse (297). Still ill, Horn tries his experiment but it goes awry, warping Horn, Rigoglio, Jahlee, Hide, Mora, Sfido, Eco, and Oreb (in dwarfish-man form) to the Red Sun Whorl rather than Green (VI, chap. 21, 312–

21). Rigoglio recognizes his old neighborhood in Nessus, but it is changed by many centuries of time. He goes inside his old house only to be stabbed by an omophagist (316). They bind the omophagist, bandage Rigoglio, and then walk upriver. Hide tells Horn he looks more like Horn in this place. They meet a man fantastically dressed who leads them to the cemetery gate (chap. 22, 324–25). They meet Badour the guard of the cemetery gate (331–32), and he takes the group around to the barbican (335–36). The lochage there writes a note for them, permission to go to the Bear Tower, where Rigoglio will be treated and they will be housed. The omophagist will be payment, and he will be put into the lion pit (337). If Rigoglio dies he will be buried as a bear keeper. He dies (chap. 23, 339). Badour and Jahlee have sex, but she bites him and he beats her for that (VI, chap. 24, 357). When they return to Blue, Rigoglio still lives but he is mindless, spiritless, a drooling husk.

~:
48: A day or two later (here two), Horn has recovered from his illness and writes in the evening about the experiment (chap. 20, 298).
49: Horn writes about the warp to the Red Sun Whorl (chap. 22, 322–25). Then Horn and Hide leave what turns out to have been an abandoned farmhouse (322; 326) and travel a short day's ride. Hide makes a shelter of sticks (326).
~:
~: Horn and Hide reach a marsh (330) so large that Hide's previous trip across took two days (341). That night (330), 30 leagues from the abandoned farm (343) yet still within Blanko territory (326), Horn writes about Badour, the guard of the cemetery (331–32; 335–37).
~:
~: Horn and Hide ride through scrub-covered hills (chap. 24, 356). Warp to Green with Jahlee, Horn, Oreb, and Hide. They find the walled village Qarya (358). Horn asks to see Sinew. They see prisoner Chenille (chap. 25, 377), who, with Auk, had attacked Qarya under threat that their inhumi masters would kill their five adopted children. They ride horses to see the lander where Horn died (375).
~: A day Jahlee is gone.
~: Second day Jahlee is gone. She comes back at night for a brief

visit (375) which Horn writes about immediately after. Hide is sleeping at the time, and he dreams he is back on Green (379).
~: This morning, the next day (379). Jahlee visits in the evening. After she flies away, two Neighbors visit at the campfire (381).
~:
~: Nearly a week later (384). Horn and Hide riding in snow overtake a woman riding a mule. Together they stop near sunset at an inn. The woman is Jahlee.

•

Appendix S2A2: Blanko and Red Harvest
Dashiel Hammett's *Red Harvest* (1928) has some deeper relevance to the Blanko situation.

In *Red Harvest,* the town is divided into multiple factions. This translates into Blanko and the other three cities.

In *Red Harvest,* when the Continental Op (the original "man with no name") is brought in to fix the problem, the detective finds that one woman, Dinah Brand, has a key in the form of explosive information. The Continental Op uses this info, which sets one faction against the other, escalating to a gang war. This use of revealing secrets to sow dissent is similar to how Horn uses a rumor of marriage along with fake side agreements to create distrust among the three other cities.

Dinah Brand is murdered as the situation spirals out of control, but in contrast to *Red Harvest,* Torda is helped along in her heart's desire for marriage with Inclito. Through this formulation, Wolfe seems to be saying that Inclito's hoarding of his estate for his daughter Mora alone causes trouble for Mora herself, since she has nightmares about being sought after for only her money; and it also means that Inclito persists in the sin of fornication, which apparently threatens more than just his personal household.

RETURN TO THE WHORL

(Volume VII)

Edition cited: Tor (hb), ISBN 978-0-3128-7314-1, 2001, 412 pp.

Dedication: "Respectfully dedicated to Teri and Al."
   Commentary: Wolfe's daughter Therese and her husband.

[Preface] To My Hosts (11)

A letter to the members of a house about the sleeping woman who can only be awakened by her father Horn. "Ask Aanvagen." Signed by Jahlee.
   Observation: A "Sleeping Beauty" angle.

1. The Bloodstained Men (13–30)

(Having dispatched some bandits, Horn has gained loot, including a bale of paper.)
   Horn is by the dead woman in her coffin, dripping blood from his slashed wrists.
   (Horn, Oreb, Jahlee, and Hide have killed nine bandits.)
   Horn is outside the building and the Long Sun Whorl is abruptly darker than night. He bandages his cuts. He walks toward the light, the only light. The light goes out, and he lies

down in the wheat to rest.

(Horn tells about Jahlee, and then quits to rest.)

* * *

(The four are trying to reach the coast. They think that when they do that, they will be north of New Viron.)

(Hide wakes him up to tell of a dream in which he seemed to walk inside a house of the Vanished People. There was also a little girl version of Mora and another little girl with yellow hair. They start to play hide and seek. He finds a doll who then becomes the new seeker. He hides under a long sofa, where there is a third girl. They are scared, and he hears the doll searching. Then he wakes up.)

Horn himself has a dream of being home at Lizard, when Sinew was an infant. A medley of times there with Nettle. He tries to affect the past by speaking to her, but he cannot say a word. He is lying on the wheat. He awakens, then goes back to sleep, thinking he is on Green prior to attacking Sinew's village.

(They meet four merchants with servants and pack animals who ask Horn to judge between them. He gets them to swear to follow his judgment and then arrests the first merchant, Nat, for failing to follow instructions.)

Observation: Horn's narration is in the third person on the Long Sun Whorl. His dream hints darkly that he led an attack on Sinew's village.

2. Great Pas's Godling (31–53)

Horn finds aid with a husband and wife. He learns he is at Endroad, near Viron on the Long Sun Whorl. He had come to their house by following the light. He wants to leave them but they say it is a darkday, with no idea when the sun will come on again.

The husband gives Horn some kernels of corn for his quest, but then the husband turns treacherous and tries to hit him from behind. Horn knocks him cold.

As he walks in the dark, Oreb joins him. Then he meets a big man who lets him handle his sword. Together they walk in the dark. The blind man settles on "Pig" as a name. They walk and come upon a godling. Horn guesses they are in a wood north of Viron, out by Blood's villa. Pig says the godlings are to drive people out to the colony worlds. Avoiding the godling, following a stream, they enter a tunnel. Coming out of it, the long sun lights up again and he sees the skylands but also the godling up close.

Observation: The Long Sun Whorl narrative maintains third person point of view established in the first chapter.

3. Justice and Good Order (54–67)

(Nat goes to Dorp, sends troopers to arrest Horn's group. They are at an inn. Jahlee needs a larger fire in her room.)

(Horn writes about bathing.)

* * *

(Oreb is back. It has been a week since the last writing. Oreb brings Horn a ring with a black stone. The stone has a picture cut into it, like a seal ring.)

(Jahlee begs to share his bed against the cold, and he does. They warp to Green, to a castle on a mountain top high above the dark clouds. No, it is a slender tower in a niche in the face of a dark red cliff.)

(Jahlee is so happy to be a real woman again that she is tempted to jump off the tower. She admits this tower is where she came when she had just learned to fly.)

(Abruptly she is gone. Horn wakes up to Azijin, one of his guards, who asks him to interpret a dream. Vlug, another guard, had the same dream. They seem to have seen the tower room.)

(The innkeeper and his wife are ill. Both have been bitten by Jahlee.)

Unusual Terms and Phrases

Leger—Dutch "army."

Mysire—seems like a compression of "my sire," used like "sir" or "monsieur." It does not appear to be a Dutch word, perhaps being in the category of Esperanto-usage among the Italophones around Blanko.

4. He Is Silk (68–91)

Pig, Horn, and Oreb force their way into a house. They meet Hound and Tansy, who set them a meal in the backyard. Tansy tells about herself and her husband. Pig says he was a trooper blinded by enemies, but also talks about "wee folk," like fairies. Particularly one named Flannan, who told him to seek new eyes in the west.

Horn goes to sleep and the three confirm he is Caldé Silk.

In a dream, Horn is in a boat, with a monster in the water below. It might be the moment before he prayed while becalmed. He is writing, rewriting, first *The Book of the Long Sun,* then *The Book of the Short Sun.*

After Horn has awakened, he and Hound get ready for their trip to Viron. While Pig still sleeps, Tansy shows Horn their shop, a general goods store. Tansy is fixing Horn's wounded arms when a villager comes in and says three men wearing headcloths are looking for Silk, too, and probably intend to harm him. As they are giving Horn a lantern, the sun goes out again.

Observation: Note the narrative shift, that Horn goes to sleep and others continue talking about him. Then his dream, which blends elements of the reader's past experience of the beginnings of Long Sun and Short Sun, when from the character's perspective he will not begin writing the Short Sun for many months, which makes the dream timeless and prophetic at precisely the moment the reader takes it to be entirely looking back.

5. Haunting Dorp (92–107)

(Horn writes in a morning to catch up. They stay at that inn for three nights. Jahlee cannot be awakened, so they rig a litter and move on to town, where now each prisoner is kept in a separate house.)

(Horn theorizes that Jahlee's spirit cannot return to her body. He must go back and bring her back, but he cannot get there without her.)

(The wife at Horn's confinement house is Aanvagen. The servant girl is Vadsig.)

* * *

(Horn dreams about being with Mora and Fava on Green, where Horn explained repeatedly about Jahlee's problem. Then the dream blends into the deadcoach dream.)

(This dream comes after he had talked with Vadsig, telling her the Outsider was the principal god on Blue, and done augury for her using sausage and brandy.)

* * *

(Next day, Vadsig brings Horn his breakfast and word that Jahlee is being kept at the house kitty-corner to the one he is in.)

(Horn manages to get the key to his room. He gets the idea to write the Jahlee letter.)

* * *

(Horn is on a tight schedule to revive Jahlee, with court day approaching in nearly a week.)

(Next day, Vadsig gets in trouble for leaving the house, but she found where Hide is being held.)

(At later meal time, Aanvagen and her husband ask Horn to interpret their dreams. The husband's dream suggests he heard Horn and Oreb sneaking through the house. Aanvagen's dream is about two girls, one light and one dark.)

(It turns out Jahlee is being held at Wijzer's house, but he is at sea. His wife Cifer has come.)

(Then Babbie arrives at the back door.)

(Cijfer shows them the Jahlee letter. Something crashes downstairs and Vadsig screams.)

Observation: We first saw Aanvagen's name in the sleeping Jahlee letter prefacing this book (VII, preface), and we first saw Vadsig's name in the editorial comment of the book before (V, chap. 5).

6. Dark Empty Rooms (108–40)

Horn, Oreb, Pig, and Hound, hiking in the darkday, come upon a vacant mansion, the ruins of Blood's villa.

Pig becomes agitated. He asks Oreb if there is a woman. Oreb replies in negatives. Pig becomes more agitated, since he thought he saw a woman but he has no eyes.

When they bring this up with Hound, he reminds them he had warned that the place is haunted by a woman. He tells them the local legend, a garbled version of ugly daughter Mucor and Patera Silk. So Horn believes Mucor still visits, and he pokes around for her. He finds her, talks to her, and sends her down to Pig.

Then Horn goes down and talks to Hound. They talk about gods. Hound wonders if the Outsider and the son of Thyone are the same god.

Horn admits that after talking with Mucor, he went looking for Hy's room. He might have found it. Pig hit a wall at that time. Pig was already there, so Horn returned.

Looking for Pig, Horn is caught by a godling. The godling calls him "holy one" and tells him enough have gone, tell the rest to stay. "Silk says it."

Myth: (Greek) The son of Thyone is Dionysius, god of wine.

7. Drinking Companions (141–56)

(Horn reports that they tried the experiment but it failed. He backs up to give all the details.)

(Horn gets Beroep to take him to Cifer's. He sits with Jahlee all night, thinking on Green to cause a warp. He sends Oreb to look for Babbie. Dawn comes and they hurry back to Beroep's.)

* * *

(Horn learns that Vadsig loves Hide.)

(Horn is searching for another inhumu to make the warp to Green possible.)

* * *

(Horn is abruptly taken to Judge Hamer's house for a preliminary hearing. He learns that his case is a capital case.)

(Hide is brought in, but he claims to be Hoof. Then he says that Horn is not really his father, but an impostor. Hamer dismisses charges against Jahlee; charges Strik with Hide's escape; releases Hide as Hoof. Cijfer bursts in to say that Jahlee has escaped.)

* * *

(Horn goes out, selling the bandit loot. To dispel the vision of Auk, he strikes up a conversation with the bar owner.)

(Jahlee comes in having fed off a drunk woman. Then Hoof comes in, newly arrived in town, and Hide comes in with bruised face and swollen eye.)

Bible: The corrupt judges of Dorp echo the Bible's Book of Judges in name and social turmoil, but nothing as direct as a Samson reference. As mentioned before, the Book of Judges is a big piece of the Bible's story between the exodus led by Moses and the kingship begun by Saul.

Observation: Horn might explain away his vision of Auk as being due to a combination of fatigue along with Horn's thief-like activity, but it might also mean that Auk died on Green, either before Horn's group visited Sinew's house (VI, chap. 24), or just at that moment when Horn saw the ghost in the tavern.

8. Sad Experience Teaches Me (157–76)

Horn shouts his own name as he stumbles back into the ruins after meeting with the godling. He gives the other two the news, admitting that this makes it sound like Echidna and Hierax won.

Hound tells him about the divine Silk.

When Pig seeks wood, Horn tells Hound what the godling told him to do and how he refuses to do it. Hound confesses his fear and dislike of Pig.

Horn tries to sleep by remembering the beginning of *The Book of the Long Sun.* He sings the haunting song of the chapter title. He dreams of the time he fetched Silk for Nettle's grandmother's deathbed.

Horn wakes up, goes up to Hyacinth's room where Pig is holed up. Horn addresses Silk within Pig, and Silk talks with him.

Then the long sun lights again.

Bible: Pig is a blinded Samson, hero from the Book of Judges. In this way, Mucor and Hyacinth are perhaps his Delilah.

Song: "Sad Experience Teaches Me" (here the chapter title, from a song first introduced in V, chap. 9, then added to in V, chap. 16) appears to be Wolfe's version of an Irish folk song called "Spanish Lady," "Dublin City," or "Wheel of Fortune." Here a new verse is put in the middle.

> *Trampin' outwards from the city,*
> *No more lookin' than was she,*
> *'Twas there I spied a garden pretty*
> *A fountain and an apple tree.*
> *These fair young girls live to deceive you,*
> *Sad experience teaches me.*
>
> *Stretched and felt before I dared to,*
> *Shinnied easy up the tree,*
> *Saw her sitting by the window.*
> *Busy as a honeybee.*
> *These fair young girls live to deceive you,*
> *Sad experience teaches me.*
>
> *I'm old now, and soon must leave you,*
> *But fairer maid I ne'er did see.*
> *Curse me not that I bereave you,*
> *I cannot stay, no more would she.*
> *These fair young girls live to deceive you,*
> *Sad experience teaches me.*

All the three songs describe the young man subsequently falling in love with a beautiful young woman as he passes by her dwelling place at various times of day and night; Wolfe compresses this into one love-at-first-sight encounter while the singer is reaching to steal an apple.

To reiterate previous points (in notes for V, chap. 9 and V, chap. 16), the line "Sad experience teaches me" comes from the Burl Ives version of "Dublin City," and Wolfe's third verse shows bits of both "Dublin City" and Campbell's version of "Spanish Lady."

In the second verse, the fruit might be inspired by a mention of apples in a version of "Spanish Lady,"

> *Ripest apples soonest rotten,*
> *Hottest love soonest cold;*
> *Young men's vows are soon forgotten,*
> *Pray, pretty maids, don't be so bold*

9. Before My Trial (177–93)

(In Dorp, Horn is now living in the house formerly belonging to Judge Hamer.)

(He questioned Vadsig, and sensing her possession, he expected the "rider" to be Jahlee or Mucor, but instead he finds both Mora and Fava. He consults with them on overthrowing the judges who rule Dorp.)

* * *

(Horn backs up to mention he warped to Green from Hamer's sellaria without an inhuma. Perhaps he was assisted by the Neighbors.)

(Oreb returns after delivering a note to Nettle.)

* * *

(Horn, clubbed during a session of Hamer's court, finds himself in that tower on the cliff face on Green. He searches it but does not find Jahlee.)

(Back at Dorp, Horn asks Oreb about Nettle. Oreb says he will go back and get a note from her.)

(Horn returns to his search for Jahlee. As he climbs down the tower, he is attacked by a cloud of inhumi. At the top of the cliff, he meets Jahlee, who is worshipped by the inhumi. He shoots one of her worshippers. They are approached by a new figure.)

* * *

(Horn sets down the story of his trial in Dorp, held in the Palace of Justice. Oreb brings Babbie. In the courtroom there is a red-faced man Horn feels he should recognize.)

Unusual Terms and Phrases

Bilocation—his word for the space-warping this guide refers to as "warp" (183).

Bible: Horn consulting spirits inside Vadsig recalls the episode of Saul and the witch of Endor. King Saul, seeking advice from the ghost of the Prophet Samuel, visits the witch of Endor in disguise (1 Samuel 28: 7-20).

The model of demonic possession as a home invasion, discussed earlier (VI, chap. 23), comes around again. Vadsig being possessed by two entities, Mora and Fava, is just like the scripture quote.

> *When the unclean spirit is gone out of a man, he walketh through dry places, seeking rest, and findeth none. Then he saith, I will return into my house from whence I came out; and when he is come, he findeth it empty, swept, and garnished. Then goeth he, and taketh with himself seven other spirits more wicked than himself, and they enter in and dwell there: and the last state of that man is worse than the first.* (Matthew 12: 43-45)

10. Through Quadrifons' Door (194–220)

Horn, Oreb, Pig, and Hound are getting closer to Viron. Horn is thinking on that song again. They pause at a pink house he remembers. They visit a manteion he had never seen. Pig admits he killed an augur and then had a religious experience, and found himself changed. Horn, as a layman, shrives Pig.

Hound asks Horn to teach him the gods by their statues.

They get to town, leaving Hound at Ermine's as they continue to Sun Street Quarter. Horn tells a story of a boy that seems to be from Silk's life. When they reach the ruins of Horn's childhood, he sends Pig away, back to Ermine's with Oreb.

Horn goes through the ruins of the manteion.

Then he walks to the Caldé's Palace. There a woman's voice from a window calls to him as Patera Silk. Then he is grabbed by Olivine, but he does not know Olivine. She seems disabled, perhaps a leper. She uses a key and the password "Quadrifons" to enter the Caldé's Garden.

Horn tells her what he knows about the god Quadrifons.

Olivine leads Horn on a task, into the palace and upstairs. He visits the room he had shared with Nettle. Olivine shows him a room he might bathe in.

Observation: The double story of Horn's letting go and Silk's coming out of grief.

Myth: (Roman) Quadrifons is an aspect of Janus, god of gates, doors, doorways, etc. The Romans associated Janus with the Etruscan deity Ani. In the Chrasmologic Writings, Quadrifons is the most holy of the minor gods (215), sometimes shown as a sort of monster combining Pas's eagle with Sphigx's lion (216).

11. My Trial (221–36)

(Now Horn is on a ship from Dorp to New Viron. He turns again to describing his trial and the overthrow of Dorp's judges.)

(He admits he felt the whole plan depended on help from Mora and Fava, that they would possess Hamer.)

(The trial begins . . .)

(On the ship, Wijzer interrupts the writing. Horn abruptly remembers him, the red-faced man, as being the one who drew him the map to Pajarocu. Wijzer tells him Marrow has died. Horn asks for his impressions of Horn's trial. They touch on highlights, including the warp to the Red Sun Whorl and the arrival of the Vanished People.)

(Horn picks up with the court arrival of the Vanished People. Then on the ship, Vadsig interrupts with her concerns about marriage. In the course of this, Horn says that the Neighbors visited the Long Sun Whorl and infected it with inhumi.)

Unusual Terms and Phrases
Ab initio—Latin phrase "from the beginning," used in law.
Testis oculatus . . . —Latin phrase "one eye-witness is worth more than ten ear-witnesses" (225).

12. Palaces (237–58)

Olivine checks in on bathing Horn. After the bath, Horn realizes she is a chem, and that her mother is Maytera Marble.

Alone, Horn goes to the room of his memory and he spends time there. Then he goes with Olivine on her task. She has a simple site for simple sacrifice, using wine for the blood and bread for the meat. He reads a paragraph from the Chrasmologic Writings. After they talk about this, Horn tells her about meeting his own father that day.

Horn meets his father Smoothbone at the ruins of the old shop and reveals himself. They go to a nearby tent bar to drink and talk. When Smoothbone says he is remarried, Horn is stunned. Smoothbone leaves the pencase for him to find.

With Olivine at the palace, Horn offers a funeral sacrifice for his body on Green. To Quadrifons and the Outsider. Olivine gives Horn one of her eyes for her mother.

At Ermine's, Horn learns that Gulo is looking for him.

Horn sleeps, wakes up, sneaks out. Walks past the night clerk arguing with a man in a headcloth. Horn forces his way into the glasshouse, kneels and prays to find Silk in this place. He hears Hyacinth and sees their reflection in the pool.

Horn gets his staff from the palace and returns to Ermine's.

Chrasmologic Writings
The citation beginning "'There, where a fountain's gurgling

waters play . . . '" is based on a passage in Book XII of Alexander Pope's translation of *The Odyssey*. When Odysseus visited Hades, he was surprised to meet the shade of his youngest comrade Elpenor, and he promised to give Elpenor's corpse a proper cremation. True to his word, Odysseus returned to Aeaea and led Elpenor's funeral rites. This quoted part is from after the funeral, where Odysseus is speaking to his men about mourning for lost friends, which poignantly links the funeral of Elpenor with the funeral for the man who died on Green.

Literature: Robert Borski points out that the scenes introducing Olivine link to Victor Hugo's novel *Les Misérables* (1862), specifically to two adjacent chapters, "Quadrifrons" [sic] and "A Rose in Misery" (Borski, *The Long and the Short of It*, p. 139). To expand a bit more, in Hugo's epic the "four faces" are not an archaic Roman god but instead four letters begging for charity, found in a packet by the lead character Marius. These letters are from different signatories, describing different scenarios, but all from the same hand. When "Rose" (actually a character named Éponine), a daughter of needy neighbors, delivers a similar note to Marius, he notices the handwriting matches the four other letters as well. This "Rose" herself is a contrast of innate beauty and behavioral degradation; education and criminality; wealth and poverty.

Observation: The surprise that Horn's father did the same thing that Horn did. Smoothbone's second wife and new family parallel Horn's relationship with Seawrack, even to the extent of having Krait as a "new" son. (There might even be a hint of generational similarity in the other direction, with Sinew having found a girl and left his father behind matching Horn going with Nettle to Blue.)

13. The Yawl (259–76)

(Horn, Jahlee, and Oreb are in a tent by New Viron, where Gyrfalcon has declared himself caldé.)

* * *

(From the tent, Horn records that when winter began, he was in Gaon fighting the Man of Han, and now winter is over and he is nearly home.)

(He slides into writing about the Red Sun Whorl, when the apprentice visited him in his cell. That was the second visit, when they warped to the Broken Court.)

* * *

(In New Viron, Gyrfalcon left him waiting for a meeting until he gave up at midafternoon.)

(On the Red Sun Whorl, he meets Merryn the witch.)

* * *

(In New Viron, Horn visits the house that had been Marrow's, and the new owner directs him to Capsicum. In turn, Capsicum sends the boy Weasel to fetch Calf to identify his brother Horn. Calf sends back a note she reads silently, then she says Marrow left Horn a boat. They go to see it and sail it a bit. She says he is in danger from Gyrfalcon. He tells her about how he and the others overthrew the judges of Dorp. The judges took advantage of the good qualities of Dorp's people; but Gyrfalcon is taking advantage of the bad qualities of New Viron's people. In its current state, New Viron could not be governed by a good person like General Mint or Silk. Either one would have to grow worse or hand leadership over to someone else.)

* * *

(Oreb reaches the boat.)

Bible: The prophet is not honored in his own hometown, as noted in scripture, "For Jesus Himself testified that a prophet has no honor in his own country" (John 4:44). Even though Horn was able to help the cities of Gaon, Blanko, and Dorp, it seems to have been a sequence of diminishing returns.

Trial in Dorp Points: The trial remains obscure, and the episode is fragmented, but at this point enough pieces have emerged to form an outline.

1. Horn in cell sees Babbie and Oreb (VII, chap. 11, 222).
2. Horn is marched to the courtroom (VII, chap. 9, 192).
3. There is poltergeist activity in the courtroom, which

means Mucor is present (VII, chap. 11, 225).
4. Windcloud the Neighbor is called as witness (VII, chap. 11, 230).
5. Nat tries to withdraw his accusation (VII, chap. 11, 233).
6. They warp directly to the Broken Court on the Red Sun Whorl (VII, chap. 13, 261). Horn, Jahlee, and Hamer are put into different cells of the Matachin Tower. The apprentice visits Horn with paper, pen, and ink. Horn proposes they visit Hamer (263). They go to Jahlee's cell and meet Merryn (266). They talk of going to see the apprentice's dog (267).
7. At Hamer's cell they convince him to convict Horn (VII, chap. 13, 275). Those from Blue warp back to Blue.
8. Babbie enters the courtroom, chases Hamer (VII, chap. 11, 228).
9. Horn owns the house that was Judge Hamer's (VII, chap. 9, 177), so the trial is over and the revolution is won.

14. Luncheon at the Caldé's Palace (277–304)

Horn, Pig, Hound, and Oreb meet with Caldé Bison at his office. Horn tells about New Viron. He makes the case for bringing Silk to New Viron. Bison makes the case for how Silk's colonization program bled Viron.

All go by floater to lunch at Bison's palace. Bison mentions Mint is in a wheelchair now.

Mint starts trying to talk sense to "Silk," but then interrupts this to speak alone with Pig in private. When Mint returns, she tells Horn about her would-be assassin and the unpopular decisions she had made, mainly the halting of the colonization.

Horn tells them that the godling told him to end colonization.

Mint tells about the little ghost. She then makes the case that he is Silk.

Horn denies it.

•

Pig Talk. When Pig says, "Nae. Save yer pother. Yer guid qife would nae be crouchy an' sae guid a leech yer ha'," it translates as, "No. Save your bother. Your good wife would not be crippled if so good a surgeon you had (as could give me sight)."

15. Home (305–17)

(Horn in yawl at Mucor's Rock, along with Hide, Vadsig, and Jahlee. Horn gives Marble the eye from Olivine.)

(Horn admits to Vadsig he is not bald.)

(Shift to Marble in the yawl under sail. She is determined to return to the Long Sun Whorl to reunite with her husband and complete the construction of their child Olivine.)

***

(Horn dreams he is back on the Red Sun Whorl and he sees a hundred black-robed women standing on the sea. He awakens and allows Oreb to fly off. He speaks to Marble, who talks about chem sleep.)

***

(Horn arrives home. He is happy to see Nettle, but he is watching for Seawrack.)

***

(Jahlee is dead. Horn found Jahlee feeding on Nettle and killed her with his hands and feet.)

(When Nettle learns Horn had brought an inhuma into their home, she is shocked to the core.)

(Jahlee tells him that Krait was her son from Sinew. Jahlee tells the secret of the inhumi, and dies.)

(This marks the end of Horn's narration.)

16. Hari Mau (318–36)

Horn is meeting with Incus prior to assisting at sacrifice. He meets again with Mint, who acknowledges that he is not Silk. She gives him the azoth that Silk had given her.

At the big ceremony, Horn tells them what the godling said.

After the ceremony, the turban-men find Horn and Pig. They

declare Silk "Rajan of Gaon." Hari Mau introduces himself. He says they came at the command of Echidna, who spoke to them in dreams. Horn agrees to go, if they first fly Pig to the West Pole.

Jump ahead to the West Pole, after the surgery, and Horn wants to visit Pig's bedside. The surgeon leads him part of the weird way, facing wind and sand, low-gravity and radiation. The surgeon tells how Great Passilk got angry at his wife and half of their children, who turned themselves into animals to escape.

Chrasmologic Writings

> *A simple way would be to admit that myth is neither irresponsible fantasy, nor the object of weighty psychology, nor any other such thing. It is wholly other, and requires to be looked at with open eyes.* (VII, chap. 16, 324)

This passage comes from most of the last part of "Epilogue, Part I" (328) in *Hamlet's Mill: An Essay on Myth & the Frame of Time* (1969) by de Santillana and von Dechend. This trippy book on measuring "deep time" through myths got a boost in popularity through John Crowley's award-winning novel *Aegypt* (1987), later known as *The Solitudes.*

Observation: The irony that Hari Maru had the same quest as Horn, but succeeded.

Myth: The detail about gods turning into animals to escape sounds like Norse Myth, perhaps limited to the Norse god Loki.

17. He Took Me with Him (337–70)

(Hoof takes up the story: After burying Jahlee, Horn and Hoof go into town to talk with Gyrfalcon. Horn talks with a lot of people. He has a dream where Scylla is talking to him from the ceiling. Horn walks the streets at night, looking for signs of inhumi.)

(Gyrfalcon sends men to bring Horn alone by force, but Horn and Babbie mess them up. Horn, Hoof, and Babbie go to

Gyrfalcon's house, where Horn hands over the corn seed from the Long Sun Whorl.)

(Back in the town, Horn finds an inhumu named Juganu and they use him for a warp to the Red Sun Whorl. In this, Oreb reveals the Scylla inside, a skinny girl with straight black hair. Juganu begins to act out, so Horn ends the trip.)

(Back on Blue, Horn tells them the task is to get Scylla out to sea in the Red Sun Whorl.)

(They take a second warp to the same ship moving down the river at night. The mate gives some trouble until the girl Scylla starts in on him.)

(Horn says Scylla possessed Oreb recently, when Incus spoke with Horn over a glass about the sacrifice [356], referring to an event occurring between chapters.)

(They go back to the yawl on Blue, deal with pirates.)

(Hoof includes information on the gods.)

(They warp again to the ship, now on the delta. They get out of the delta and the girl Scylla starts calling for hours. Then women appear, singing.)

(They return to Blue. Hoof talks to Scylla with mixed results. Juganu tells him the new job is to take the girl to her grave in the city of the Red Sun Whorl.)

Unusual Terms and Phrases
Samru—The ship of the Red Sun Whorl is named after the bird of immortality in Persian myth.

18. How He Came to Blue (371–82)

Horn visits Pig who now has one blue eye. Pig wants to continue on with Horn, but Horn is against it, and Pig needs recovery time. Silk in Pig talks to Horn directly.

Jump ahead to Hari Mau helping Horn in the lander. They talk about the sights. Horn tries to say he was fobbed off on Hari Mau by Viron, and goes through many details.

Jump ahead to after he has landed on Blue and is being

transported in a horse-drawn vehicle.

Unusual Terms and Phrases
Tonga—a light carriage.
Myth: The Norse god Odin gave his eye to Mirmir, the giant guarding the Well of Wisdom, and thereby gained wisdom.

19. The Last Time (383–97)

(On Blue they plan their next warp. They go to Capsicum's house.)

(The warp is not forthcoming, so Horn describes the Red Sun Whorl, then Juganu describes inhumi courtship rituals. Horn uses this to talk about prostitutes and prisoners at the city they are going to. Then they warp to the top of the lander of the torturers.)

(Horn appeals to the apprentice, who takes them to a crypt. They release the Cilinia spirit fragment from existence.)

(The apprentice wants to show the visitors his dog. Hoof is against it, but Horn needs to find Juganu. They see the dog, then struggle with Juganu, wherein they warp back to Blue. Juganu leaves them abruptly.)

Observation: It appears that inhumi around humans are locked in reproductive mode, similar to prostitutes among GIs, or the way Le Guin's Winter people look at humans in *The Left Hand of Darkness* (1969). This angle emerges when Horn talks to Juganu about prostitutes on the Red Sun Whorl; people playing a "wedding night" role that has been taken out of context, a shortcut that is unfulfilling.

20. The Wedding (398–408)

(Horn reads the entrails of the sacrifice. First, he tells them they belong to Blue and to the Outsider. They hurry through the wedding as inhumi swarm to attack. The attack comes as bride and groom start back down the aisle.)

(The ensuing melee sees human heroism and human

treachery.)

(Afterwards, in private conversation with Patera Remora, Horn confesses that he stirred up the attack in the hope that he would be killed, but he thought it would be personal and private, against him alone.)

(Remora gives him a talk on his suicidal thinking. Has him read a passage from the Writings.)

(This passage releases Horn's spirit from Silk's body.)

Observation: A wedding and then a funeral, or an exorcism.

Plato's Cave: In the course of his travels, Horn comes to see that, far from being empty, the universe outside the Long Sun Whorl is full of real gods. Horn says, "We have other gods here [on Blue] already. There is a Scylla greater than the one we knew, for example" (VII, chap. 20, 399), referring to the Mother. In this way, while we initially take the gods of the Long Sun Whorl as being exaggerated shadows of mere mortals, we learn that in fact they are diminished shadows of true gods like the Mother and others.

Afterword (409–12)

(Notes on the composition of the text. The first two volumes as written by the former Rajan, the third volume's chapters involving Old Viron and the West Pole being filled in by the editorial team of Daisy, Hide, and Vadsig.)

(Following the interview with Remora, the one-eyed man was seen only by Daisy, who provides notes on that meeting: the former Rajan is laying in supplies in the yawl, preparing for a trip with Oreb, Seawrack, Marble, and Nettle.)

(He asks Daisy to make his goodbyes to Hide and Hoof. He killed their father, and he does not want to face the sons.)

(They are sailing away to find Pajarocu. To take a lander to the Long Sun Whorl.)

(In a final note, someone at some later time sees the Long Sun Whorl growing smaller as it begins moving out of the star system, and prays "good fishing" for the five.)

Chrasmologic Writings

"Though trodden beneath the shepherd's heel, The wild hyacinth blooms on the ground" (VII, chap. 20, 408) comes from a fragment of a poem by Sappho, famed poetess of Lesbos: "As on the hills the shepherds trample the hyacinth under foot, and the flower darkens on the ground."

APPENDICES FOR RETURN TO THE WHORL

Appendix S3A1: Timelines for Return to the Whorl

Timeline from Long Sun Whorl to Gaon

Day: Note

1: Horn awakens in room with coffin (VI, chap. 8, 127; VII, chap. 1, 13). It is midday, but soon the Long Sun goes out: his first experience of a darkday (VII, chap. 1, 15). As he falls asleep in a field of wheat, Oreb finds him (19). He dreams of returning to Lizard (26). After awakening, he follows a light to a house and meets the nameless couple there (chap. 2, 31). The corn seed man gives him the grains of maize he requests (37), but then threatens him. Continuing along, Horn meets Pig (42). They avoid a godling guarding a bridge (52). One league later, the skylands light up. At Endroad village (chap. 4) they meet Hound and Tansy. Horn goes to sleep. Hound, Tansy, and Pig agree that Horn is really Silk. Pig goes to sleep. Horn has a dream mixing future and past (chap. 4, 83–85).

2: There is light in the morning for a while, then darkday (91). Hound sets out for Viron with Horn and Pig. They find the ruins of Blood's villa (VII, chap. 6, 109). Pig sees the ghost of a woman. Hound tells "The Story of the Ugly Daughter." Horn contacts Mucor. Godling meets Horn outside (137). Horn returns to Hound and Pig (chap. 8, 157). He thinks he has been away from New Viron for a year (169). Horn figures out that Pig is being ridden by Silent Silk (173).

3: Walk to Viron (chap. 10, 194). They visit northern manteion (197). Horn goes alone to Sun Street manteion (211). He visits the location of Smoothbone's old shop, meets Smoothbone and has a drink with him at a tavern (VII, chap. 11, 249–52). Returning alone to the old shop, he finds a pen case on the step (VII, chap. 11, 230). He goes to the Caldé's Palace where he meets Olivine (chap. 10, 213). Coadjutor Gulo goes to Hound's room at Ermine's looking for Silk (chap. 12, 255; chap. 16, 319). Horn sleeps a few hours at Ermine's, then goes to the fish pond, looking for Silk (chap. 12, 256–57). After this Horn goes to the Palace to get the knobbed stick he had left there while visiting the room of Horn and Nettle (258).

4: Group goes to meet Caldé Bison at his office (VII, chap. 14, 277). Bison invites them to lunch, a floater-ride away at the Palace. Horn convinces Mint he is not Silk. Group goes to perform sacrifice at 3 o'clock in the Grand Manteion. Scylla possesses Oreb when Incus through his glass asks Horn to assist at the sacrifice (between chapters; revealed VII, chap. 17, 356). Mint gives Horn the azoth (VII, chap. 16, 320). He says he conversed with the godling two nights before (326). Hari Mau meets him (328) after searching Viron for only eleven days (VII, chap. 18, 380). Horn agrees to go with them to Gaon if they can first get an eye operation for Pig at the West Pole (chap. 16, 330).

~:

~: Pig's surgery is successful (330). To visit him, Horn must cross leagues of difficult terrain. Horn meets Pig (chap. 18, 371), cuts the bandage, and sees that Pig can see (372). Then he talks to Silk about how he cannot take Pig (and Silk) to Blue (374). Finally Horn goes to the lander which sets out for Gaon (374–82).

Timeline to Dorp and then to New Viron

Day: Note

1: Horn, Hide, Jahlee, and Oreb encounter nine bandits on the road (VII, chap. 1, 14) and prevail against them in combat. Horn has a new bale of paper (13).

2: They hoped to reach the coast this day, but do not (20). Once they reach the coast, Hide says they will be at least a week north of New Viron. Hide has a dream involving Mora and Fava (21).

3: Riding downhill all day, they meet four merchants on the road, including Ziek and Nat (28). The four plead with Horn to judge their argument. He has them swear they will follow his words. They agree. He orders them to travel separately, starting with Nat who will go ahead first. Nat refuses. Horn orders the others to arrest him, and they do so. Horn intends to release him the next morning.

4: Horn releases Nat, who races ahead to Dorp, from which he sends troopers to arrest Horn and group (VII, chap. 3, 54). The troopers and their prisoners are at an inn. Dinner and bath (55).

5: It is snowing hard when Oreb returns, bringing Horn a black ring (56). Jahlee shares bed with Horn and they warp to a slender tower on Green (58).

6: At the snowbound inn, Horn's guards tell him about the weird dreams they had (62–64), and he tells them about warp. The innkeeper and his wife are both "sick" from Jahlee feeding (67). Jahlee becomes stuck in Green, her body on Blue locked in a coma-like sleep.

7: They arrive at Dorp and are under house arrest in three different houses (chap. 5, 92). Horn meets Vadsig, servant girl. He has a dream of being with Mora and Fava in jungle on Green (94–95).

8: It is Molpsday and they say his trial will be on Sphigxday (98). Horn finds where Jahlee is held and writes a letter in her name for Oreb to place in her window.

9: Tarsday. Horn goes out after midnight (98), comes back before dawn. In the morning, Aanvagen and Beroep ask Horn to interpret their weird dreams (101–103). Cijfer, while coming to visit Horn, sees Babbie on street (105). Horn convinces Beroep to take him to Cijfer's after dark (chap. 7, 141). There he tries experiment to wake Jahlee, but fails.

10. Hieraxday. Horn returns to Beroep's place at dawn and writes about the night's adventure (143). Vadsig brings word from Hide (144). At night Horn is taken to Hamer's house

for a preliminary hearing. He has been in Dorp for 8 days (according to Horn, presumably counting from meeting the merchants) or 6 days (by Beroep's count, presumably counting from the inn) (148). [Note: if B is counting from Day 7 then three days must be inserted between Day 7 and Day 8.] After being beaten unconscious (chap. 7, 150; chap. 9, 185), Horn searches for Jahlee from Hamer's sellaria (chap. 9, 183). He warps to Green, to the mid-cliff tower again (185), and finds Jahlee is being worshiped. They are met by a Neighbor who talks them into going back to Blue (191). During Horn's preliminary hearing, Jahlee awakens in Dorp and escapes the house (chap. 7, 153). At Beroep's place, Horn talks with a possessed Vadsig (chap. 9, 177), then he goes out, wakes jeweler, sells some jewelry (raising money to buy guns to enable rebellion), and goes to the tavern (VII, chap. 7, 153). Hide goes to Strik's house, is beaten, then goes to tavern (chap. 9, 182). In tavern Horn sees a ghostly vision of Auk, then talks to the tavern owner and son (chap. 7, 153). Jahlee comes in, drunk. Hoof comes in. Hide comes in. The Neighbors make themselves known to Horn (chap. 9, 185).

11: Thelxday? Wijzer and Wapen ready others for rebellion (chap. 11, 221).

12: Phaesday? Wijzer and Wapen ready others for rebellion (221).

13: Sphigxday, day of the trial (chap. 5, 98). Horn in a waiting cell sees Babbie and Oreb (chap. 11, 222). He is marched to the courtroom in chains (chap. 9, 192). There is poltergeist activity in the courtroom, presumably due to Mucor (chap. 11, 225). A Neighbor named Windcloud testifies as witness (230). Nat tries to withdraw his accusation (233). Horn warps a group (probably all the people in the courtroom, but at least Horn, Jahlee, Hamer, and Wijzer) directly to the Broken Court at the Citadel on the Red Sun Whorl (chap. 13, 261). Horn, Jahlee, and Hamer are put into different cells of the Matachin tower. The apprentice visits Horn with paper, pen, and ink. Horn proposes they visit Hamer (263). They go to Jahlee's cell and meet Merryn (266). They talk of going to see the apprentice's dog (267). Hamer is scared and wants to dismiss the charges against Horn, but Jahlee and Horn order him to convict Horn, in order to start the uprising (VII, chap. 13, 275). They return to Blue. Hamer convicts. Babbie enters the courtroom, chases Hamer (chap, 11, 228). The uprising begins.

~:

~: The rebellion of Dorp, wherein the judges are overthrown by 100 men with guns (221) and many more with knives and clubs (222). There are plans to supply food but the rebellion does not last long enough (222).

~:

~: Horn now living in Hamer's house, given to him by the town (chap. 9, 177). He writes about talking to a possessed Vadsig on Day 10. Then he goes to court.

~: Oreb returns from trip to Lizard, where he delivered a note to Nettle (chap. 9, 184).

~: Next day Horn is writing about immediate conversation with Oreb, which ends when Oreb goes out to get a written reply from Nettle (185). Horn writes about his search for Jahlee on Green (187).

~:

~: Days since Horn last wrote (191). Oreb not yet returned (192). They plan to sail next day. He writes about the trial.

~: At night Horn and group put out in ship to sail to New Viron (chap. 11, 221).

~: Sailing to New Viron (221). Oreb on ship, no mention of reply from Nettle (227).

~: Horn writing about sailing to New Viron (221) and about his trial in Dorp.

~:

~: Detained by contrary winds within sight of New Viron (VII, chap. 13, 259).

~: Make port at New Viron in morning (259).

~: In a tent on the beach with Jahlee (260). Winter nearly over. When it began, Horn was in Gaon fighting the Man of Han (261).

~: Hoof visits tent again, goes to Lizard.

~: Horn spends morning waiting at Gyrfalcon's (264).

~: Horn goes to Marrow's former house, then to Capsicum (267).

~: "When I wrote yesterday evening" (276).

~:

~: At first light Horn sets out from New Viron for Mucor's Rock, with Jahlee, Hide, and Vadsig (VII, chap. 15, 305). In the evening he writes about it.

~:
~: At Mucor's Rock, Horn gives Marble her new eye (306–307).
~: Horn talks with Marble alone, explaining the source of the eye.
~: Marble, who is going to the Long Sun Whorl, joins group on sailboat and sails away (VII, chap. 15, 309).
~: Horn awakens from dream set on the Red Sun Whorl (312).
~: Horn arrives at Lizard with Marble and Jahlee (313). He finds Jahlee feeding on Nettle and he kills Jahlee. He writes about it and quits writing.
~:
~: (Written by Hoof.) Horn and Hoof go to New Viron (VII, chap. 17, 337). Horn walks through town, talking to people. Horn and Hoof sleep on their boat but Horn is troubled in night (339).
~: Horn and Hoof stay at Calf's. Horn dreams of Scylla (339).
~: Horn stays up late (searching town and taverns for an inhumu).
~: Horn stays up late.
~: Horn stays up late. Meeting with Gyrfalcon (340–43). Horn gives him the corn seeds from the Long Sun Whorl.
~: They find the inhumu Juganu and take him out in boat for warping to the Red Sun Whorl (343) where they hire the riverboat *Samru* before warping back to Blue (348).
~: Three or four hours after daylight, they warp to the Red Sun Whorl, back onto the *Samru* (353). It is night, not long before dawn, a half-day upriver from the delta (354). Shortly after sunrise they warp back to Blue and deal with some pirates closing in. When the pirates shoot Hoof, Horn uses the azoth to kill a few pirates and cut the bow off their vessel (358). Horn bandages Hoof, makes potato soup (359). When it is nearly dark Juganu flies back to feed off the pirates (358). They warp to the Red Sun Whorl, onto the *Samru* that is now in the delta (363). They meet Great Scylla (365). They warp back to Blue, where it is night (366). Hoof talks with Scylla in Oreb and learns a lot.
~: Three days sailing to New Viron (VII, chap. 19, 383).
~: From Capsicum's house at 2 p.m., Horn, Hoof, Juganu, and Oreb/Scylla warp to the Red Sun Whorl. They arrive in the uppermost level of the Matachin Tower (387). They send Juganu to summon the torturers' apprentice (389). The boy

comes up alone. Hoof is surprised that this boy is younger than his own sixteen years. On the Red Sun Whorl this time Horn looks like Silk (388). Horn asks the apprentice to take them to Cilinia's grave (390). He does and they open her casket, allowing her restless ghost to find peace (391–92). Then the apprentice takes them to see his dog, but first they search for Juganu. They find him in a cell with Tigridia (395). They leave him there, go downstairs to visit the dog. Back at Tigridia's cell they fight with Juganu who does not want to return. They force him and warp back to Blue (397).

~:

~: (Written by Daisy.) The wedding of Vadsig and Hide, and the attack of 1000 inhumi (VII, chap. 20, 398–401) on first warm day of summer (402). Afterward Patera Remora talks to Horn and releases the spirit of Horn (401–408).

~: [Several days.]

~: Silk, Nettle, Seawrack, Marble, and Oreb set sail for Pajarocu, bound for the Long Sun Whorl.

~: [Two years later.]

~: Daisy writes the latter part of the Afterword in the second year of Blazingstar's caldéship. The Long Sun Whorl seems to be leaving the star system.

·

Appendix S3A2: Co-Authorship

As *The Book of the Short Sun* begins, Horn tells about how much his wife Nettle contributed to the composition of *The Book of the Long Sun* as a silent partner, ultimately amounting to co-authorship. Through this admission of the true labor that went on behind the scenes, Horn seems to be missing her help in composing this new work, effectively admitting that he never has written alone.

But he is not really alone, as it becomes increasingly clear that there is something of Silk to him, thus he is co-authoring again, and this time Silk is the silent partner. But then this mutates when we learn that Horn died on Green, and Silk might be the one who is writing a book for the first time, a biography of a person he hardly knows. This fuzzy authorship changes the autobiography into biography. That is, the author of the Odysseus volume is actually two men, one who failed in his quest by dying, and the other a new widower who failed in his attempt at suicide.

Then there is the editorial squad of four (Hide, Daisy, Hoof, and Vadsig). They first peep in the text at volume V (chap. 5). The more dramatic move is in volume VII when Hoof and Daisy write late chapters on things they experienced first-hand, but the real bombshell is when they admit at the end of volume VII that Daisy, Hide, and Vadsig wrote all of Horn's few days on the Long Sun Whorl. This "DHV text" changes the biography into pastiche. The young people have no first-hand experience of the Long Sun Whorl, they only know it through *The Book of the Long Sun,* so they are presumably mining *The Book of the Long Sun* for any details to flesh out their narrative. Their other sources are oral items told to them by the one-eyed man, and the text written by the one-eyed man, so naturally they are mining *The Book of the Short Sun* itself for hints on what happened to "Horn" on the Long Sun Whorl. To give just one example, the power of the song "Sad Experience Teaches Me" in volume VII is all from the two verses of the song by the one-eyed man in volume V. Every little scrap of foreshadowing by the one-eyed man is an element to be fleshed out, completed by someone else. That includes every cryptic statement about Pig and Olivine. Whereas *The Book of the Long Sun* is presumably raided by the editors for details on people like Mint and Bison who are purely literary characters for the editors.

·

Appendix S3A3: The Quest to Find Silk
Three parties are trying to find Silk on the Long Sun Whorl:

1. Horn, selected by faction leaders of New Viron after they had read *The Book of the Long Sun.*

2. Hari Mau, instructed by Echidna in a dream after he had

read *The Book of the Long Sun.*

3. Pig, searching for a year, has Silent Silk trapped inside him.

Hari Mau is the clear winner, since he gets Horn inside the body of Silk, which is a perfect match for the Silk of the book, since Horn is the author of that book.

Then there is a possible fourth party in Seawrack. She was given to Horn (or Horn was given to her), but she may be only using Horn to get to the Long Sun Whorl. After Horn ditches her, she starts singing to Silk, who confuses her with Hyacinth. Her goal might be Silk, or the Long Sun Whorl. Among readers there is speculation about Seawrack carrying one spiritual entity or another, for example, Hyacinth (scanned at the pool) or Kypris. Borski thinks it is Kypris (*The Long and the Short of It,* p. 117–19).

From the beginning of *The Book of the Short Sun,* Horn tells his readers that he has failed to bring Silk. In the course of the first volume, we come to see that he looks a lot like Silk; through the second volume, we see Horn's spirit rehoused in Silk's body; but the third volume proves to be paradoxical for being a pastiche, meaning that the reader must choose between a static state (the situation remains as it was in volume II) or a read-between-the-lines "wild card" state (where the situation continues to change as the story rolls out).

The static state means that the reader knows the situation and watches the character fumble in his way toward understanding the situation. The static state means that the reader remains locked in seeing Horn's denial and madness. Every time Horn says, "I'm not Silk," from the first volume to the third, is Horn's irrational denial; every time Horn tries to find Silk is worse than Diogenes with his lantern, so much worse that it trips over the line from "deep philosophy" to "clear madness."

But what if it is not denial, not madness?

One way this might be is if Horn woke up in Silk's body and there was no trace of Silk's spirit: the "house" of Silk's body was empty except for Horn's spirit. So Horn is not in denial: he is telling the truth.

The madness charge might resolve as easily as that. From the beginning on the Long Sun Whorl, where he asks the nameless husband and wife (VII, chap. 2), to the mid-point at Gaon, when he is writing letters to every city-state he can (V, chap. 1, 18), Horn is searching for Silk because he knows that he does not have him. Someone else might be possessed of a copy of Silk, in one form or another.

With this in mind, the DHV text shows Horn discovering that Pig has a copy of Silk trapped in him (VII, chap. 8). Horn wants to help Pig, but it might not be purely altruistic, since Horn might get a copy of Silk within himself through optical transfer. The source of Pig's copy is questionable, however (the issue being if Silent Silk is free of Pas, or not), and presumably Horn would prefer to find an earlier copy. A potentially cleaner copy would be the one made at Ermine's pool. Horn attempts Ermine's pool (VII, chap. 8). Later he bargains with Hari Mau for Pig's operation (VII, chap. 16). Horn gives his eye and travels to see Pig face to face (VII, chap. 18).

These hypothetical attempts by Horn show a decline in standards which would fit a reasonable rise in desperation. That is, the original goal was to fetch 44-year-old Silk. To that a second goal was added, to obtain a copy of 23-year-old Silk from the pool, with the warning that it might be Passilk. And then a third goal, that of securing a copy of Silent Silk, which is not only more likely to be contaminated by Pas, it is also guaranteed to have 20 years of godhood baggage. The third goal does not replace the others, but all three quests run simultaneously.

·

Appendix S3A4: Modes of the Hero

The Book of the Short Sun is a dual-track tale that starts in the middle of things and runs along in tandem to double conclusion.

Untangling it and setting everything into linear order, the hero goes through a number of distinct modes. In the first mode he is like Odysseus, with his odyssey set before him and a Siren bride along the way. When he gets to Green, however, his mode is more like Joshua in the Book of Judges, warlord in a strange new land; yet when he fails, he is like Spartacus.

The third mode is a complex one. The hero is initially Orpheus, the fresh-grieving widower, and something like Don Quixote, an obvious madman. When he sacrifices his eye, he takes on a layer of the Norse god Odin that persists through the other volumes.

The Rajan of Gaon is like King Solomon, the third king of Israel. Famously wise, with a harem of wives and mastery over supernatural beings.

Incanto at Blanko, a man with no name, is a lesser leader but still a cunning warrior, perhaps a King David, the second king of Israel.

The sixth mode is the homecoming failure as King Saul.

1. Setting forth as Odysseus
2. Warlord of Green as Spartacus
3. Widower of Endroad as Orpheus, Don Quixote, and Odin
4. Rajan of Gaon as King Solomon
5. Incanto at Blanko and on Green as King David
6. Homecoming failure as King Saul

•

Appendix S3A5: About the Ending
The ending has Silk, Seawrack, Marble, Nettle, and Oreb heading to the Long Sun Whorl.

Silk and Nettle must go because they know the secret of the inhumi.

Marble must go to reunite with her husband and with him complete the construction of their daughter Olivine.

The releasing of Horn's spirit from Silk's body is similar to the situation in David Lindsay's *A Voyage to Arcturus* (1920), where two men, Maskull and Nightspore, set out from Earth at the start of the novel, but only one arrives to quest across the alien planet, until the twist ending of the penultimate chapter:

> "What is this Ocean called?" asked Maskull, bringing out the words with difficulty.
> "Surtur's Ocean."
> Maskull nodded, and kept quiet for some time. He rested his face on his arm. "Where's Nightspore?" he asked suddenly.
> Krag bent over him with a grave expression. "You are Nightspore."
> The dying man closed his eyes, and smiled.
> Opening them again, a few moments later, with an effort, he murmured, "Who are you?"
> Krag maintained a gloomy silence.
> Shortly afterward a frightful pang passed through Maskull's heart, and he died immediately.
> Krag turned his head around. "The night is really past at last, Nightspore.... The day is here."
> Nightspore gazed long and earnestly at Maskull's body. "Why was all this necessary?" (chap. 20)

It turns out that Nightspore had been a silent passenger in Maskull's body for most of the novel, and emerged only when Maskull died.

In a 1973 interview, Wolfe recommends *A Voyage to Arcturus* with the caveat "I despise its philosophy" (Wright's *Shadows of the New Sun,* 17) and Wolfe speaks of it again in a 1992 interview (ibid, 104).

There is another piece of literature that, while far shorter, has many more points of similarity to *The Book of the Short Sun*: Lewis Carroll's "The Hunting of the Snark" (1876). This nonsense poem uses eight sections to describe a group of ten persons, led by the Bellman, on a hunt for a legendary beast in an unknown land.

The first section talks about the sailing across an uncharted sea, not unlike Horn's voyage to Shadelow continent. One of the hunters is the Baker, who loses his name early on, and answers to a variety of names including "Ho," points that make him seem like a close match to the Horn/Silk narrator. Among the hunters there is a non-human, the Beaver, who is surprisingly capable, rather like Babbie the hus. The fifth section involves the Jubjub bird, which is somewhat similar to the Pajarocu bird. The sixth section is all a weird court case involving dream, which finds an echo in Horn's court trial in Dorp. The dissolution of the successful hunter (the Baker) in the end, anticipates the dissolution of Horn after successfully getting Silk back to New Viron.

Wolfe made reference to Lewis Carroll many times, but perhaps the only link to "The Hunting of the Snark" is in Wolfe's essay "The Bellman's Wonder Ring" in *Clarion SF* (1977). Joan Gordon annotates it as "Wolfe ponders the difficulty of teaching professionalism in writing" (Gordon, Joan. *Gene Wolfe.* 108). He does this using many quotes from the poem.

APPENDICES FOR THE SHORT SUN SERIES

APPENDIX SSA1: ALL TIMELINES (SEVEN)

Timeline 0. History

Years Ago: Note
2,500: Eco's estimate for passage of time since Roger left the Red Sun Whorl (VII, chap. 22, 325).
1,900: Hide's estimate (325).
1,000: Horn's guess at a minimum (325).
1,000: The Vanished People vanish.

100: Around a century ago, the Long Sun Whorl arrives in the Short Sun system; the Neighbors visit the Long Sun Whorl, introducing inhumi.

20: Colonists establish New Viron. Horn is 15 years old (VII, chap. 14, 279). Subsequent colonists include convicted criminals as well as laborers, small farmers, and craftsmen (281). Horn and Nettle marry. Sinew, conceived on the Long Sun Whorl, born on Blue.

16: Conjunction (first time). Blazingstar comes to New Viron from the Long Sun Whorl, possibly in same lander as Gyrfalcon (V, chap. 1, 24).

15: Horn and Nettle move to Lizard Island. Seawrack born (a year or two older than Hoof and Hide). Jahlee bites Sinew.

14: Hoof and Hide born (16 years old in the end). Gaon established (VII, chap. 18, 379).

12: On the Long Sun Whorl ten or twelve years ago (VII, chap. 4, 78), Silk steps aside for Mint to become caldé of Viron (VII, chap. 14, 287). Eight days later the long sun goes out, the first darkday (290). Mint is shot and crippled by a would-be assassin (292).

10: Conjunction (second time). Blanko fights Heleno and Poliso (VI, chap. 2, 45–48).

9: Wijzer comes to Blue from the Long Sun Whorl (V, chap. 4, 117). On the Long Sun Whorl, Horn's half-brother Antler is born.

6: Five or six years ago, Marble and Mucor move out of New Viron (V, chap. 3, 76).

5: Bricco is born (VI, chap. 2, 40).

4: Conjunction. On the Long Sun Whorl, Hound and Tansy return to Endroad from Viron (VII, chap. 4, 72).

3: Two or three years ago, Horn talked to a man of New Viron who boasted about his beautiful slave girl (V, chap. 4, 99–100)

1: Sinew finds shrine on Howling Mountain (V, chap. 1, 38).

0: Fava goes to Soldo to visit relatives (VI, chap. 2, 38). Two years ago. In Dorp, Vadsig starts working at Beroep's house (VII, chap. 7, 145). On the Long Sun Whorl, Pig starts walking to the West Pole (VII, chap. 4, 75).

Timeline 1. From New Viron to Green

Day: Note

1: The mainshaft of the papermill had split when Hide tells Horn a ship is coming to their island (V, chap. 1, 19). It is the five faction-leaders of New Viron—Blazingstar, Eschar, Gyrfalcon, Marrow, and Patera Remora. After they leave, Horn has dinner with his family to explain what he has sworn to do (26). Horn accepts the mission to go to the Long Sun Whorl and return with Silk to New Viron. Sinew thinks the real plan is to bring Pas to Blue (35). Conjunction with Green is due in two years (38). Horn leaves at night, while Nettle, Hoof, and Hide are asleep (42).

2: Day (44), Horn prays for wind, and at sunset is visited by a leatherskin (chap. 2, 59–61).

3: New Viron. Horn talks to Remora about gods of the Vanished People (56–58). Remora flatly refuses to tell anything about Maytera Marble (chap. 3, 75).
4: Horn's ship is robbed of some valuables while he is at Marrow's (74).
5: To Mucor's Rock, two days' worth of travel (78), where Marrow had said even with a good wind it would take all day.
6: Midmorning arrive at Rock.
7: Next morning, Mucor has returned from visiting Silk (chap. 4, 95). Gift of book for Marble, gift of Babbie for Horn. Back to New Viron, arrive in time for dinner with Wijzer at Marrow's. Horn spends night at dock. Horn's plan is to sail north 100 leagues, then cut west (122).
8: Sail at dawn (chap. 5, 126), pass Lizard after noon (127). Beginning of six weeks' sailing time (128).
50: A pirate boat gives chase (132), and Horn kills a woman shooting at him. She falls into the sea. To avoid the pirates Horn begins sailing west.
51: The next morning Horn finds blood on deck (134). Babbie gets small tree at sunset (138). They hear the Mother's song, probably sorrowing for Seawrack's wound.
52: Next dawn they find a low green island (141). Babbie had been on board for several weeks (141). Inland the great flat creature attacks them. They return to sloop to find Seawrack (145). She leaves, comes back with the Mother (chap. 6, 152–53). Storm comes at night (160), tears up vegetative green island (161). A crustacean man thing comes onboard for a tense, enigmatic encounter (161). The following days they sail west-northwest. This period includes the best and happiest hours of his life, "days of gold" spent with Seawrack (170).
~:
57: Nearly a week later (163) they meet another ship (166) and learn of young man (Sinew) searching for Horn. Captain Strik says they should sail north by northwest for Pajarocu (167). News of an island with good water two or three days west (169). At night Krait comes aboard (chap. 7, 174), feeds off of Babbie.
58: Wind picks up before noon (186), and they sight island before sundown (187).
59: Next day, hiking the island, Horn and Seawrack talk of

making a home there after bringing Silk to New Viron (188–89). They discover ruins of Vanished People (chap. 8, 191–92). Horn falls into pit, becomes unconscious (chap. 9, 196).

~: Horn sleeps for at least three days (196).
62: Night of no sleep.
63: In the morning Krait finds him (197), leaves.
64: Day Horn licks the dew and is visited by a Vanished Person who gives him a ghostly visit with Nettle (203).
65: Late afternoon when Krait visits a second time (203). They bargain, then Krait helps him escape (210). They meet Babbie. Night when they reach sloop (218).
66: Foggy morning. Krait arrives, guides them to Seawrack who is singing (chap. 10, 228). She is skittish, and Krait urges Horn to hold her and make her sing (231). She sings a few notes and he rapes her. That night they spot fires on the shore (242). Seawrack goes into the water (251).
67: Horn waits around all day and at sundown Seawrack drives a fish on board. She gives him the Neighbor ring (253).
68: They make landfall on the western continent at the Land of Fires. At noon they reach the little river (V, chap. 11, 259), but it is near dark when they meet He-pen-sheep and family (261). He-pen-sheep tells Horn of a big river to the north (281). At night Horn goes out to meet Neighbors (263–64; 266–72) and meets Horn the Neighbor (273). On the way back he kills a breakbull (273).
69: Back on sloop (276). Horn must cut anchor line at night to avoid being dragged under (279), all because Krait had gone off hunting during his watch.
70: They see He-pen-sheep again, who gives them head of breakbull (280).
~:
~: Fish strip the flesh from it in a few days (chap. 12, 292).
~:
~: They find the mouth of the river (293).
~:
~: Three days sailing up the river (293).
~: First day at Wichote (293).
~: Second day at Wichote. Probably the day Horn and Seawrack try to enlist the shaman who brags of having put an invisible devil upon the trail of others (V, chap. 5, 137).
~: Third day at Wichote. Day after shaman episode, on the

riverbank with Seawrack, Horn feels there are three of them, but it turns out he is counting Babbie (137).
~: Market day, and that night Krait says he found Pajarocu, ten days away (323).
~:
~: First week (323)
~: Meet Sinew coming down from Pajarocu (329).
~:
~: Presumably three days later they arrive in Pajarocu. During the day a few men show Horn and group the lander (351). At night, Seawrack senses night hunters, and Horn recognizes one of the men who had shown the lander visiting a nearby boat. He sees this man subdue the foreign woman there but does not understand it as such.
~: Market day. Horn figures out the lander is from Green (352). There is a meeting that night at the tavern Bush about the foreign woman who was bitten (353).
~: Horn and Sinew spread the word about the lander (359). That night Sinew and Horn plan method to leave Seawrack downstream.
~: The lander leaves with Horn, Sinew, and Krait (360–61). Trip probably takes weeks.
~:
~: Krait tries to divert lander to Long Sun Whorl but cannot (374).
~:
~: Krait visits Horn and tells him he has sabotaged one of the two inhumi needlers (373).
~:
~: Last fight on lander, Krait and inhumi barricaded in nose, Horn and group break in but are too late anyway (380).

❖ ❖ ❖

Timeline 2. From Green to the Long Sun Whorl

Day: Note
1: Horn and the other humans are in the underground prison. After Krait's brief visit, Horn gets the sewer job from a Neighbor (VI, chap. 1, 20).

2: Searching all day for the sword and light lost at the end of the sewer job (chap. 6, 101). At night he finds the light (102).
3: At night Horn finds the sword (103).
4: Horn goes back to free Sinew and the others (chap. 5, 91).
5: Perhaps the next day, unable to persuade the 100 men to retake the lander, Horn agrees to lead them in search of colonists (chap. 8, 120). They go north.

~:
~: They fight a small settlement. There are 69 men left. Horn goes back to retake the lander and 45 men follow him. The hike back takes 4+ days.

~:
~: They fight their way to the landing spot, but the lander is gone. Down to 27 men (123). They fight inhumans, human slaves of the inhumi, and Horn is wounded.

~:
~: Krait, who had joined them, is wounded. The inhumans pursue them into the jungle.

~:
~: Krait and Horn left behind. Krait dies in jungle (V, chap. 16, 374; VI, chap. 5, 81; chap. 8, 124).

~:
~: Horn catches up with group.

~:
~: They travel far.

~:
~: They find deserted settlement with a ruined lander (125). They work at repairing the lander.

~:
~: Sinew finds a woman at one of the settlements they raid and turns against Horn (126).

~:
~: One by one Horn's men die.

~:
~: Horn is riding the three-horned beast when he is mortally wounded (V, chap. 3, 94).

~:
~: Fava goes to Soldo again and hears rumors of Bricco (VI, chap. 2, 43).

~:
~: As Horn is dying, his last two men leave, taking both

the sword and the light. Horn uses the ring and a female Neighbor takes his spirit to place in a body on the Long Sun Whorl. The body had belonged to Silk (VI, chap. 8, 127).

Timeline 3. From Long Sun Whorl to Gaon

Day: Note
1: Horn awakens in room with coffin (VI, chap. 8, 127; VII, chap. 1, 13). It is midday, but soon the Long Sun goes out: his first experience of a darkday (VII, chap. 1, 15). As he falls asleep in a field of wheat, Oreb finds him (19). He dreams of returning to Lizard (26). After awakening, he follows a light to a house and meets the nameless couple there (chap. 2, 31). The corn seed man gives him the grains of maize he requests (37), but then threatens him. Continuing along, Horn meets Pig (42). They avoid a godling guarding a bridge (52). One league later, the skylands light up. At Endroad village (chap. 4) they meet Hound and Tansy. Horn goes to sleep. Hound, Tansy, and Pig agree that Horn is really Silk. Pig goes to sleep. Horn has a dream mixing future and past (chap. 4, 83–85).
2: There is light in the morning for a while, then darkday (91). Hound sets out for Viron with Horn and Pig. They find the ruins of Blood's villa (VII, chap. 6, 109). Pig sees the ghost of a woman. Hound tells "The Story of the Ugly Daughter." Horn contacts Mucor. Godling meets Horn outside (137). Horn returns to Hound and Pig (chap. 8, 157). He thinks he has been away from New Viron for a year (169). Horn figures out that Pig is being ridden by Silent Silk (173).
3: Walk to Viron (chap. 10, 194). They visit northern manteion (197). Horn goes alone to Sun Street manteion (211). He visits the location of Smoothbone's old shop, meets Smoothbone and has a drink with him at a tavern (VII, chap. 11, 249–52). Returning alone to the old shop, he finds a pen case on the step (VII, chap. 11, 230). He goes to the Caldé's Palace where he meets Olivine (chap. 10, 213). Coadjutor Gulo goes to Hound's room at Ermine's looking for Silk (chap. 12, 255; chap. 16, 319). Horn sleeps a few hours at Ermine's, then goes to the fish pond, looking for Silk (chap. 12, 256–

57). After this Horn goes to the Palace to get the knobbed stick he had left there while visiting the room of Horn and Nettle (258).

4: Group goes to meet Caldé Bison at his office (VII, chap. 14, 277). Bison invites them to lunch, a floater-ride away at the Palace. Horn convinces Mint he is not Silk. Group goes to perform sacrifice at 3 o'clock in the Grand Manteion. Scylla possesses Oreb when Incus through his glass asks Horn to assist at the sacrifice (between chapters; revealed VII, chap. 17, 356). Mint gives Horn the azoth (VII, chap. 16, 320). He says he conversed with the godling two nights before (326). Hari Mau meets him (328) after searching Viron for only eleven days (VII, chap. 18, 380). Horn agrees to go with them to Gaon if they can first get an eye operation for Pig at the West Pole (chap. 16, 330).

~:

~: Pig's surgery is successful (330). To visit him, Horn must cross leagues of difficult terrain. Horn meets Pig (chap. 18, 371), cuts the bandage, and sees that Pig can see (372). Then he talks to Silk about how he cannot take Pig (and Silk) to Blue (374). Finally Horn goes to the lander which sets out for Gaon (374–82).

Timeline 4. Gaon

Day: Note
~: The Rajan arrives in Gaon (VII, chap. 18, 382).
~: Oreb flies off for over a year, or "the better part of a year" having the adventure of "The Night Chough" among others. Nine months (270 days) seems most likely.
~:
1: The Rajan begins writing (V, chap. 1, 18).
2: Second day of writing (18).
3: Writing about the day or two before Horn left Lizard (19).
4: The Rajan formalizes court of Gaon (25).
~:
8: Three days without writing (33).

9: Evening of above day or next day—three asterisk break (34).
10: Writing about decision not to return with the five (39).
11: Writing personal notes to his family (40).
12: Two farmers quarrel over a strip of land (41).
13: Writing of how long it has been since Horn left Lizard with regard to his sons, the Rajan writes, "Between birth and twenty, a year is an eternity" (46). Suggests it has been one year.
14: To do nothing is a talent (V, chap. 2, 49).
15: The Rajan puts paint on one lens of his glasses, presumably to hide his lost eye (54).
16: Writing about talking to Remora about gods (56).
17: Writing about prayer on sloop (58).
~:
21: A few days later, the Rajan takes a day off and writes (66).
22: Writing about Marrow (69).
23: Writing about the robbery (74).
24: Writing about sailing to Mucor's Rock (77).
~:
27: Three days since he last wrote (78). Very late (93).
28: Writing the Tale of Pajarocu (V, chap. 5, 95).
29: Green bigger than a man's thumb last night (106). [Possibly late July, i.e., one year before conjunction?]
30: Inhuma caught last night (108).
31: Writing about Wijzer (123).
32: Writing about the accusation that *The Book of the Long Sun* is fiction (124).
~:
35: Not touched for three days, very late—near midnight (125). Storms have nearly wiped out the date palms.
36: Writing about the Thing on the Green Plain (126).
37: A visitor gives the Rajan a book on herbs called *The Healing Beds* (129).
38: Perhaps the next day, "In my last session" (131).
39: Mention of a shaman Horn and Seawrack met (137).
40: Writing about arriving at the Green Plain (140).
41: Elephant sacrifice (145).
42: Ambassadors from Skany (V, chap. 6, 147).
43: Writing about meeting Seawrack (156).
~: The Rajan goes to Skany and stays "most of the summer" (158), which sounds like a period of 60 to 80 days.

During this time an inhumu or inhuma is burned at Skany (V, chap. 10, 241).
103: Estimate 60 days in "A long while since" (158).
104: Writing about the second day with Seawrack (159).
105: Writing about meeting Captain Strik (167).
~:
107: Two days have passed (169).
108: Writing about leaving Strik's ship (V, chap. 7, 171).
109: Writing about meeting Krait on the sloop (173).
110: Writing about inhumi in general (183).
111: Writing about the rest of the night after Krait left the sloop (184).
112: Writing about sailing to the island of the pit (186).
113: Writing about hiking on the island (187).
114: Writing about falling into the pit (V, chap. 8, 191).
115: Writing about meeting Krait in the pit (chap. 9, 195).
116: Writing about negotiations with Krait and rescue (202).
117: A fortune-teller at court a few days ago (211).
118: Barsat comes to court to ask protection from the Vanished People (212).
119: Writing about going back to the sloop (213).
120: The Rajan goes hunting (215).
121: Writing prologue for a tangent on cattle (216). Weather sultry for at least a week (221).
122: The Rajan dreamt that Oreb was back (223).
123: The Rajan goes hunting again (chap. 10, 225).
124: Writing about the semi-feral Seawrack (227).
~:
131: A week later—a week of heat and terrible, violent storms (233). The Rajan writes of "The account I began last year" (234).
132: Writing about when Seawrack sang (234).
133: Writing about the day after (239).
134: The Rajan buries an inhumu and two inhuma (240).
~:
136: Writing about trying to return to normal (241).
~:
~: The big storm (245), the climax of conjunction. This should be about two years after Horn left Lizard.
~:
~: August 2nd—conjunction is past (246).

APPENDIX SSA1: ALL TIMELINES (SEVEN) 203

~: August 3rd—rain all day (251).
~: August 4th—writing about the Land of Fires (V, chap. 11, 255).
~: August 5th—writing about meeting He-pen-sheep (260).
~: August 6th—writing about bedding down at camp (263).
~: August 7th—Barsat and the Vanished People's house event (265). A Neighbor (Windcloud) gives the Rajan an ancient chalice.
~: August 8th—writing about meeting the Neighbors (266).
~: August 9th—writing about the hike back to camp (273).
~: August 10th—writing about sailing again (277).
~:
~: The War break (V, chap. 12, 283). Weeks or months later. The Rajan has been wounded (283) while upriver (299). He is suicidal (284).
~: The Rajan's forces pushed back again, nearly to town (287). The Rajan visits the front with Evensong, who interprets as he questions fresh prisoners on top of the elephant (288).
~: The Rajan sends Bahar and Namak downriver, Bahar to buy food, and Namak to hire mercenaries (290). The front is now an hour's ride away (291).
~: Four prisoners kill themselves (291).
~: The Rajan talks to prisoners (292).
~: The Rajan writes that it is nearly two years since Horn found the river to Pajarocu (293), which was in Fall. Truce agreed upon between Gaon and Han.
~: Hanese forces driven back (293).
~: Armorer visits in morning (298); the Rajan has secret mission for next day.
~: The Rajan rides elephant through impassable brush (299). Three boatloads of food from Bahar arrive (303).
~: Pounding rain (302). The rainy season has started (303). Winter wheat should have been planted (303).
~:
~: The Rajan returns after two days of rain—near 8 p.m. (304). They unearth Jahlee (V, chap. 13, 313).
~: The Rajan writes the next day about unearthing Jahlee (313).
~:
~: Four days after unearthing Jahlee, three days after last writing (322).
~: The Rajan in bed much of day (336).

~:
~: Away a long while. In another week the rainy season should end (V, chap. 14, 343). Oreb returns (346) after more than a year (369). [Implies he left before the rainy season the year before.]
~: Two a.m. (V, chap. 14, 355). The Rajan and Evensong in escape boat, heading down river (V, chap. 15, 363). Scylsday (365). They travel about one day down the river before stopping.
~: The war is over, won for Gaon, and so the inhumi are searching for the Rajan (V, chap. 16, 371). The Rajan leaves river, abandoning Evensong (376), trying to go northwest (377).
~:
~: Last time the Rajan ate was two days before (377). He meets a forest god (378).
~:
~: The Rajan meets Brother and Sister (378).
~: Second day with Brother and Sister.
~: Third day with Brother and Sister.
~: Fourth day with Brother and Sister.
~: The Rajan leaves Brother and Sister, they follow (379).
~: In morning, Brother and Sister are gone (379). At night the Rajan dreams of Pig and Hound (379).
~: The Rajan reads most of manuscript (380).

The total time the Rajan is in Gaon seems to be about a year. Oreb seems to have left shortly before the Rajan started writing, but the writing might have begun not on the first day in Gaon but after three months. The longer Oreb lingers, the more feathers he drops.

Timeline 5. Blanko

Day: Note
   1: Horn in village of woodcutter Cugino (VI, chap. 1, 16), located one day south of Blanko (VI, chap. 2, 37). He has soup (VI,

chap. 1, 24). A good woman fixes his torn robe (23).
2: Horn arrives in Blanko.
3: Horn starts writing, meets Inclito (VI, chap. 1). Nearly a week since he heard any news from Gaon (29). Agrees to take the name Incanto. Goes to dinner at Inclito's house. First storytelling game. Horn sleeps at the stationer's shop. Dreams of being back in pit (chap. 3, 58).
4: Horn spends most of daylight hours sleeping off the heavy meal in alley barrel (chap. 5, 74). A week or 10 days since leaving Evensong (75). In the morning he talks with Mora (76). She says Inclito will write a letter to him, and she promises one when she gets home from palaestra (78). Middle of afternoon in barrel (chap. 2, 35). Horn gets letter from Inclito, urging him to come and stay at the house (83–84). Then there is a letter from Fava. He goes to the palaestra, gives coachman a note to Inclito saying he would come not that day but the next (96). Night at stationer's (chap. 5, 74). Midnight (75).
5: Morning (83). Afternoon ride with the girls Mora and Fava to house (chap. 6, 104). Night (93). Second story telling game (110). First experience of warping to Green (chap. 9, 145; 156), a "dream" interrupted by the Cook (chap. 13, 194).
6: After midnight, a nightmare awakens him at Inclito's house and he writes about searching for sword on Green (chap. 5, 90). He questions the kitchen maid (93). He tries to sleep again, writes more. Maid brings tea and tarts (94). Writing about night of Day 5 (chap. 9, 133). Dawn. Fields about to be plowed for winter wheat (140). Breakfast. Sacrifice of a young bull reveals message from the Outsider and the Mother that the horde of Soldo has already set out to invade Blanko (chap. 10, 151). Dinner with two messengers (148).
7: In the morning, Mora rides off with message (chap. 11, 171). Inclito goes after her, and both are captured (181). Horn goes to Blanko, as ordered (chap. 12, 185). Horde (20 cavalry, 96 infantry) marches forth—first day of Mobilization (presumably). They nearly reach the last plowlands before they camp (186).
8: Second day of march halts at night on word that enemy is near, at saddle. Vivo arrives with additional troops, bringing the total to 250. At night in camp, Horn writes about morning of Day 7 (171). Then on patrol he

meets mercenaries at saddle (180–82). He writes of this immediately after.

9: Horn trades himself for Inclito (chap. 12, 191). He is held with Fava, whom the mercenaries think is Mora (192). They huddle in the snow and warp to Green, taking along Captain Kupus's company of 200 men. Horn warps Oreb over, where he appears the size of a four-year-old child (chap. 13, 203). Horn offers to return them to Blue if they leave the service of Soldo. They refuse and he leaves them in the prison cell, going into the sewer.

10: After midnight Valico finds them there and says the whole camp is sleeping (chap. 14, 210). Horn has Fava think of Duko's palace in Soldo, and they warp there (215). Fava, Valico, Horn, and Oreb meet Duko and sue for peace. He refuses. The other mercenaries follow Oreb in and try to shoot the Duko but then they are back on Green (220). Kupus pledges to follow him (chap. 15, 226). They take Sfido's needler (230). They fight a worm in the sewer that kills Chaku and Teras (224). They fight against the City of Inhumi, intending to kill all inhumi (chap. 16, 236–38). When they warp back to Blue they find Chaku and Teras alive (224), but Fava has died in the snow.

11: Writing about Day 9 (chap. 12, 183). With Kupus's 200 and another group that arrives, Horn now has more than 300 fresh mercenaries.

~:

~: Horn returns to Blanko, stays with Atteno the stationer (chap. 13, 192). He writes more about Day 9. The tenth of the month is only three days distant (195). The citizens are raising money (chap. 14, 220), but they want to cheat the mercenaries (222).

~:

32: Blanko celebrating in evening at news that Olmo, besieged by Soldo, requests aid from Blanko. Horn is still at Atteno's, where he writes about Day 9 and the mercenaries in the sewer on Green (chap. 15, 224). Sfido arrives at door, first seen in ten days (227).

33: After midnight, Horn writes of Sfido's visit (226). During the day, Sfido and Horn drill Blanko troops.

34: Sfido and Horn drill Blanko troops (chap. 16, 238).

35: Horn writing of Days 33 to 34. Rimando arrives with

letter (preface) from Inclito (238), dated 27th day of the Mobilization. [Which means Day 34+, if Mobilization starts on Day 7.] Olmo has fallen (238).

~: March two days to outpost location, where they dig ditches, sew thousands of sacks.

38: Preparations for battle (241–43). Colbacco brings new men from the south, including Cugino and a boy who looks like Hoof and Hide (244).

39: Morning—snowing (243). Horn at farmhouse. Dinner with the old woman (244).

40: Battle of Blanko. A few days after the letter (VI, chap. 17, 255). At this point the mercenaries had been with them almost half a month (253). Winter wheat is tall enough to hide a boar. Retreating Blanko troopers, 50 to 100, pass through after dawn (chap. 16, 244–45). Inclito is in the rearguard, which stays (245). The battle begins an hour or two past noon (258). Horn and Terzo parlay. Second attack comes 15 minutes later (chap. 18, 270). They have shattered the Dragoons (269). Horn forms up a group to give chase into the hills, in the morning (272). He writes about seeing a boy who looks like Hoof and Hide on Day 38.

41: Midnight, writing a bit about the battle of Blanko, promising to write more next day (chap. 16, 245). Old woman visits and Horn realizes she is Jahlee (248). After midnight, the second attack (VI, chap. 16, 246; chap. 18, 272) by the Ducal Bodyguard who forded the river (272–73). They wipe out the Bodyguard (269). Morning after battle (274). Horn takes a large force and moves to catch up with Inclito. Evening in the hills, not at the farmhouse (chap. 17, 247). Writing about the Battle of Blanko (248–67).

42: Catch up with Inclito on second day (chap. 18, 275). A representative from Novella Citta arrives with 450 troopers (chap. 17, 267).

43: Horn writes "The End and Afterward" (chap. 18, 270–73) about the battle. He hopes to find an altar the next day (274).

44: Horn writes about the morning of Day 41 (274), then reports that on the current day they discovered the Duko disguised among their prisoners (275). Horn interviews Duko Rigoglio, and Mucor appears in the campfire smoke to say that Babbie has returned (280).

45: Oreb finds an altar of the Vanished People on a hill to north (chap. 19, 281). Horn plans experiment to visit Green the next night (283). Horn meets Cuoio and sees he is Hide. They sit on Fava's gravestone (293). Hide says Horn left Lizard about three years ago (294). Baletiger episode, in which Cuoio kills game driven toward them. Horn becomes ill that night (chap. 20, 297). Horn writes about the day (chap. 19, 281).

46: Morning at Jahlee's farmhouse (297). Still ill, Horn tries his experiment but it goes awry, warping Horn, Rigoglio, Jahlee, Hide, Mora, Sfido, Eco, and Oreb (in dwarfish-man form) to the Red Sun Whorl rather than Green (VI, chap. 21, 312–21). Rigoglio recognizes his old neighborhood in Nessus, but it is changed by many centuries of time. He goes inside his old house only to be stabbed by an omophagist (316). They bind the omophagist, bandage Rigoglio, and then walk upriver. Hide tells Horn he looks more like Horn in this place. They meet a man fantastically dressed who leads them to the cemetery gate (chap. 22, 324–25). They meet Badour the guard of the cemetery gate (331–32), and he takes the group around to the barbican (335–36). The lochage there writes a note for them, permission to go to the Bear Tower, where Rigoglio will be treated and they will be housed. The omophagist will be payment, and he will be put into the lion pit (337). If Rigoglio dies he will be buried as a bear keeper. He dies (chap. 23, 339). Badour and Jahlee have sex, but she bites him and he beats her for that (VI, chap. 24, 357). When they return to Blue, Rigoglio still lives but he is mindless, spiritless, a drooling husk.

~:

48: A day or two later (here two), Horn has recovered from his illness and writes in the evening about the experiment (chap. 20, 298).

49: Horn writes about the warp to the Red Sun Whorl (chap. 22, 322–25). Then Horn and Hide leave what turns out to have been an abandoned farmhouse (322; 326) and travel a short day's ride. Hide makes a shelter of sticks (326).

~:

~: Horn and Hide reach a marsh (330) so large that Hide's previous trip across took two days (341). That night (330), 30 leagues from the abandoned farm (343) yet still within Blanko territory (326), Horn writes about Badour, the guard

of the cemetery (331–32; 335–37).
~:
~: Horn and Hide ride through scrub-covered hills (chap. 24, 356). Warp to Green with Jahlee, Horn, Oreb, and Hide. They find the walled village Qarya (358). Horn asks to see Sinew. They see prisoners Auk and Chenille (chap. 25, 377), who had attacked Qarya under threat that their inhumi masters would kill their five adopted children. They ride horses to see lander (375).
~: A day Jahlee is gone.
~: Second day Jahlee is gone. She comes back at night for a brief visit (375) which Horn writes about immediately after. Hide is sleeping at the time, and he dreams he is back on Green (379).
~: This morning, the next day (379). Jahlee visits in the evening. After she flies away, two Neighbors visit at the campfire (381).
~:
~: Nearly a week later (384). Horn and Hide riding in snow overtake a woman riding a mule. Together they stop near sunset at an inn. The woman is Jahlee.

Timeline 6. To Dorp and then to New Viron

Day: Note
1: Horn, Hide, Jahlee, and Oreb encounter nine bandits on the road (VII, chap. 1, 14) and prevail against them in combat. Horn has a new bale of paper (13).
2: They hoped to reach the coast this day, but do not (20). Once they reach the coast, Hide says they will be at least a week north of New Viron. Hide has a dream involving Mora and Fava (21).
3: Riding downhill all day, they meet four merchants on the road, including Ziek and Nat (28). The four plead with Horn to judge their argument. He has them swear they will follow his words. They agree. He orders them to travel separately, starting with Nat who will go ahead first. Nat refuses. Horn

orders the others to arrest him, and they do so. Horn intends to release him the next morning.

4: Horn releases Nat, who races ahead to Dorp, from which he sends troopers to arrest Horn and group (VII, chap. 3, 54). The troopers and their prisoners are at an inn. Dinner and bath (55).

5: It is snowing hard when Oreb returns, bringing Horn a black ring (56). Jahlee shares bed with Horn and they warp to a slender tower on Green (58).

6: At the snowbound inn, Horn's guards tell him about the weird dreams they had (62–64), and he tells them about warp. The innkeeper and his wife are both "sick" from Jahlee feeding (67). Jahlee becomes stuck in Green, her body on Blue locked in a coma-like sleep.

7: They arrive at Dorp and are under house arrest in three different houses (chap. 5, 92). Horn meets Vadsig, servant girl. He has a dream of being with Mora and Fava in jungle on Green (94–95).

8: It is Molpsday and they say his trial will be on Sphigxday (98). Horn finds where Jahlee is held and writes a letter in her name for Oreb to place in her window.

9: Tarsday. Horn goes out after midnight (98), comes back before dawn. In the morning, Aanvagen and Beroep ask Horn to interpret their weird dreams (101–103). Cijfer, while coming to visit Horn, sees Babbie on street (105). Horn convinces Beroep to take him to Cijfer's after dark (chap. 7, 141). There he tries experiment to wake Jahlee, but fails.

10: Hieraxday. Horn returns to Beroep's place at dawn and writes about the night's adventure (143). Vadsig brings word from Hide (144). At night Horn is taken to Hamer's house for a preliminary hearing. He has been in Dorp for 8 days (according to Horn, presumably counting from meeting the merchants) or 6 days (by Beroep's count, presumably counting from the inn) (148). [Note: if B is counting from Day 7 then three days must be inserted between Day 7 and Day 8.] After being beaten unconscious (chap. 7, 150; chap. 9, 185), Horn searches for Jahlee from Hamer's sellaria (chap. 9, 183). He warps to Green, to the mid-cliff tower again (185), and finds Jahlee is being worshiped. They are met by a Neighbor who talks them into going back to Blue (191). During Horn's preliminary hearing, Jahlee awakens in Dorp and escapes the house (chap. 7, 153). At Beroep's place, Horn talks with a possessed Vadsig (chap. 9, 177), then he goes out, wakes jeweler, sells some jewelry (raising money to buy guns to enable rebellion), and goes to the tavern (VII, chap. 7, 153). Hide goes to Strik's house, is beaten, then goes to tavern (chap. 9, 182). In tavern Horn sees a ghostly vision of Auk, then talks to the tavern owner and son (chap. 7, 153). Jahlee comes in, drunk. Hoof comes in. Hide comes in. The Neighbors make themselves known to Horn (chap. 9, 185).

11: Thelxday? Wijzer and Wapen ready others for rebellion (chap. 11, 221).

12: Phaesday? Wijzer and Wapen ready others for rebellion (221).

13: Sphigxday, day of the trial (chap. 5, 98). Horn in a waiting cell sees Babbie and Oreb (chap. 11, 222). He is marched to the courtroom in chains (chap. 9, 192). There is poltergeist activity in the courtroom, presumably due to Mucor (chap. 11, 225). A Neighbor named Windcloud testifies as witness (230). Nat tries to withdraw his accusation (233). Horn warps a group (probably all the people in the courtroom, but at least Horn, Jahlee, Hamer, and Wijzer) directly to the Broken Court at the Citadel on the Red Sun Whorl (chap. 13, 261). Horn, Jahlee, and Hamer are put into different cells of the Matachin tower. The apprentice visits Horn with paper, pen, and ink. Horn proposes they visit Hamer (263). They go to Jahlee's cell and meet Merryn (266). They talk of going to see the apprentice's dog (267). Hamer is scared and wants to dismiss the charges against Horn, but Jahlee and Horn order him to convict Horn, in order to start the uprising (VII, chap. 13, 275). They return to Blue. Hamer convicts. Babbie enters the courtroom, chases Hamer (chap, 11, 228). The uprising begins.

~:

~: The rebellion of Dorp, wherein the judges are overthrown by 100 men with guns (221) and many more with knives and clubs (222). There are plans to supply food but the rebellion does not last long enough (222).

~:

~: Horn now living in Hamer's house, given to him by the town (chap. 9, 177). He writes about talking to a possessed Vadsig on Day 10. Then he goes to court.

- ~: Oreb returns from trip to Lizard, where he delivered a note to Nettle (chap. 9, 184).
- ~: Next day Horn is writing about immediate conversation with Oreb, which ends when Oreb goes out to get a written reply from Nettle (185). Horn writes about his search for Jahlee on Green (187).
- ~:
- ~: Days since Horn last wrote (191). Oreb not yet returned (192). They plan to sail next day. He writes about the trial.
- ~: At night Horn and group put out in ship to sail to New Viron (chap. 11, 221).
- ~: Sailing to New Viron (221). Oreb on ship, no mention of reply from Nettle (227).
- ~: Horn writing about sailing to New Viron (221) and about his trial in Dorp.
- ~:
- ~: Detained by contrary winds within sight of New Viron (VII, chap. 13, 259).
- ~: Make port at New Viron in morning (259).
- ~: In a tent on the beach with Jahlee (260). Winter nearly over. When it began, Horn was in Gaon fighting the Man of Han (261).
- ~: Hoof visits tent again, goes to Lizard.
- ~: Horn spends morning waiting at Gyrfalcon's (264).
- ~: Horn goes to Marrow's former house, then to Capsicum (267).
- ~: "When I wrote yesterday evening" (276).
- ~:
- ~: At first light Horn sets out from New Viron for Mucor's Rock, with Jahlee, Hide, and Vadsig (VII, chap. 15, 305). In the evening he writes about it.
- ~:
- ~: At Mucor's Rock, Horn gives Marble her new eye (306–307).
- ~: Horn talks with Marble alone, explaining the source of the eye.
- ~: Marble, who is going to the Long Sun Whorl, joins group on sailboat and sails away (VII, chap. 15, 309).
- ~: Horn awakens from dream set on the Red Sun Whorl (312).
- ~: Horn arrives at Lizard with Marble and Jahlee (313). He finds Jahlee feeding on Nettle and he kills Jahlee. He writes about it and quits writing.
- ~:

~: (Written by Hoof.) Horn and Hoof go to New Viron (VII, chap. 17, 337). Horn walks through town, talking to people. Horn and Hoof sleep on their boat but Horn is troubled in night (339).
~: Horn and Hoof stay at Calf's. Horn dreams of Scylla (339).
~: Horn stays up late (searching through town and taverns for an inhumu).
~: Horn stays up late.
~: Horn stays up late. Meeting with Gyrfalcon (340–43). Horn gives him the corn seeds from the Long Sun Whorl.
~: They find the inhumu Juganu and take him out in the boat for warping to the Red Sun Whorl (343) where they hire the riverboat *Samru* before warping back to Blue (348).
~: Three or four hours after dawn, they warp to the Red Sun Whorl, back onto the *Samru* (353). It is night, not long before dawn, a half-day upriver from the delta (354). Shortly after sunrise they warp back to Blue and deal with some pirates closing in. When the pirates shoot Hoof, Horn uses the azoth to kill a few pirates and cut the bow off their vessel (358). Horn bandages Hoof, makes potato soup (359). When it is nearly dark Juganu flies back to feed off the pirates (358). They warp to the Red Sun Whorl, onto the *Samru* that is now in the delta (363). They meet Great Scylla (365). They warp back to Blue, where it is night (366). Hoof talks with Scylla in Oreb and learns a lot.
~: Three days sailing to New Viron (VII, chap. 19, 383).
~: From Capsicum's house at 2 p.m., Horn, Hoof, Oreb/Scylla, and Juganu warp to the Red Sun Whorl. They arrive in the uppermost level of the Matachin Tower (387). They send Juganu to summon the torturers' apprentice (389). The boy comes up alone. Hoof is surprised that this boy is younger than his own sixteen years. On the Red Sun Whorl this time Horn looks like Silk (388). Horn asks the apprentice to take them to Cilinia's grave (390). He does and they open her casket, allowing her restless ghost to find peace (391–92). Then the apprentice takes them to see his dog, but first they search for Juganu. They find him in a cell with Tigridia (395). They leave him there, go downstairs to visit the dog. Back at Tigridia's cell they fight with Juganu who does not want to return. They force him and warp back to Blue (397).
~:

~: (Written by Daisy.) The wedding of Vadsig and Hide, and the attack of 1000 inhumi (VII, chap. 20, 398–401) on first warm day of summer (402). Afterward Patera Remora talks to Horn and releases the spirit of Horn (401–408).
~: [Several days.]
~: Silk, Nettle, Seawrack, Marble, and Oreb set sail for Pajarocu, bound for the Long Sun Whorl.
~: [Two years later.]
~: Daisy writes at least the latter part of the Afterword in the second year of Blazingstar's caldéship. The Long Sun Whorl seems to be leaving the star system.

APPENDIX SSA2: THE DIVINE TWINS

There is a deep pattern in the Indo-European tradition about the "Divine Twins." In the Greek example of Castor and Pollux, one twin is mortal and the other is immortal. Perhaps this is translated into Romulus and Remus, where Remus dies (is mortal) and Romulus becomes a god (is made immortal).

The Book of the Short Sun has divine twins in Horn and Silk. One dies and one is a god.

The pattern goes beyond this one set. There is also Sinew and Krait, Fava and Mora, even the natural twins Hoof and Hide.

In Horn's relations with Krait and Sinew, where Krait is the evil twin of Sinew, there is irony in how the two conflicts are resolved: Horn goes back to save Krait and Krait dies in his arms, achieving atonement; whereas Horn goes back to beat Sinew and Horn receives a fatal wound that is later atoned for by Silkhorn as a part of Horn's long farewell to his life.

APPENDIX SSA3: OF THE GODS (II)

In Mainframe

Pas is restored; Echidna, Scylla, and Hierax have been erased.

The status of Kypris is not given. There is plenty of Hyacinth-related sadness from Silk that might spill over into Kypris.

On Blue

An Echidna-in-snake is in Gaon. The Scylla-in-Oreb is a more recent arrival.

There are details which might be taken to suggest there is a Kypris in Seawrack, the strongest one being Silk's emotional confusion of his wife Hyacinth and the Siren. There is also the physical pattern of missing arms: in the Long Sun series Maytera Rose lost her arms after being possessed by Kypris, and in the Short Sun series Seawrack loses her arm in a mysterious amputation. If Seawrack contains Kypris, it would be an excellent reason for the Mother, a goddess of Blue, to get her a ride back to the Long Sun Whorl to find Silk.

Gods of the Vanished People on Blue

The Mother, a sea goddess.

The forest god met by the Rajan in the wilderness between the Nadi and Cugino's village.

The Outsider, who visits the sacrifices at Mucor's Rock (V, chap. 3) and the hilltop altar Oreb found (VI, chap. 19).

Gods of the Vanished People on Green

Goddess of Purity, represented by an altar and statue at the beginning of the sewers below the City of Inhumi (VI, chap. 4, 64). Horn's magic light seems to be a gift from this goddess (64), but he says it was "no doubt" from the Neighbor who led him there (VI, chap. 5, 91).

Gods of the Red Sun Whorl

Scylla "also a sea-monster of the Red Sun Whorl" (VI, character list). This Greater Scylla seems to have been the idol of Cilinia as a child.

The Outsider

Previously we have traced in the Outsider various elements of Saturn, Jesus, and God the Father (Appendix LSA4). Now two more gods are added to the mix: the Greek Dionysus and the Norse Odin.

After Horn talks to Hound about two obscure gods, the Son of Thyone (Dionysus) and the Outsider (VII, chap. 6, 125), Hound wonders if they are the same god (133).

Silk with Oreb had earlier been identified as being an avatar of the Outsider (IV, chap. 6, 96–97), but when the character has sacrificed one eye, this is an incident alluding to Odin, which becomes stronger when the character travels under various aliases, just as Odin did.

Dionysus and Odin share a shamanistic character, a trait that Wolfe seems to explore again and again.

APPENDIX SSA4: THE STORY ORPHAN ANNIE TOLD GENE WOLFE

There was a conversation at a convention, where Wolfe talked about "Orphan Annie" telling him stories. (I'm trying to find another witness to this conversation.)

Wolfe said his mother hired a chore girl from the orphanage. She was named Annie. She told stories that really impressed Wolfe. One story seems to have been about a rogue planet arriving near Earth, with demonic aliens swimming across space to invade (which clearly has relevance to the Short Sun series). Some time later, Wolfe was surprised to find that the story Annie had told him was in a pulp magazine.

Thus, there is a clue that Wolfe was inspired by an oral version of a story in the pulps. Over the years, my attempts to identify Annie's pulp story by way of internet searching proved inadequate, but in 2021, while looking for something else, I stumbled upon the detail that Wolfe only discovered the pulps after he had read the new book *The Pocket Book of Science Fiction* (1943). With this new information, I resorted to the brute force method of examining tables of contents for science fiction pulps from 1941 to 1945: *Famous Fantastic Mysteries* (Wolfe's favorite, according to the interview with McCaffrey), as well as *Amazing Stories, Planet Stories,* and *Thrilling Wonder Stories.*

As a result of this effort, it seems like the story in question is the Ray Cummings novel *A Brand New World* (1928), which appeared entirely within the September 1942 issue of *Famous Fantastic Mysteries.*

Now, *A Brand New World* does not have aliens swimming through space (they use silver spheres), which would explain why my search for "space-swimming aliens" led nowhere. But the alien girl "Zetta" can leap so high she clears an orange tree and it looks like she is flying. "Face toward the ground, white hair waving behind her, arms outstretched, with the folds of her drapery robe opened fan-shaped, fluttering like wings."

Another curious point, related to the leap-flying, is that the aliens of the other world are incredibly light in weight. For example, Zetta is described: "by her appearance she would have weighed some ninety or a hundred pounds. Zetta weighed eighteen pounds." Later we learn that women "weighed twenty or twenty-five pounds . . . men might weigh about thirty pounds."

Eighteen-pound Zetta, the alien girl who flies by leaping, is a love interest of the narrator.

Zetta is trying to warn pre-spaceflight Earth against the aggressive rivals of her faction on the rogue planet. This other faction is the one that later invades Earth.

Conjunction between the two worlds is every 17 months.

After the war, the alien world leaves our solar system (chapter 21). It turns out to be more of a vast ship.

Zetta stays behind and later bears a son to the human hero (chapter 22).

While the aliens do not swim between the worlds, they have technology that produces infernal effects. For example, weird weapons that allow "infrared creatures" to come to Earth in form and sound, which is rather close to demons swimming in from space.

In further detail, the crimson radiance causes "red

madness." The aliens speak of "this unreal subworld" and later "the infrared world." They "think that the infrared is perhaps the evil nature of man held submerged." Two cases give vivid example:

> *"A murmur was coming from it—a myriad tiny growls and screams! The crimson sounds! The red things lurking around me responded to it! Or were they making the sounds? I could not tell. They seemed rushing out from the unseen into visibility—searching—One seemed almost to be plucking at me!"*

and

> *"The red things were howling around me. One came up— a great crimson shadow. It seemed to be condensing into the form of a man. Suddenly I heard myself laughing . . . It looked like me! . . . It was trying to get into my body!"*

It seems particularly pertinent that the hellish world produces devilish doppelgangers, exactly like the situation in Wolfe's work where the inhumu Krait is revealed to be a replica of human Sinew.

The crimson radiance, at "very weak intensity," is used as a cloak of invisibility, but also the melee blows from a cloaked person have "infrared" aspects, causing sunburns and sun blindness.

In any event, I believe I have traced down Wolfe's anecdote as linking to this early novel. But again, notice how he first heard the story from a mysterious young woman, the chore girl orphan Annie.

BIBLIOGRAPHY FOR THE SHORT SUN

Bible. Joshua (VI, chap. 8)
———. Judges (Appendix S1A2; VII, chap. 7)
———. 1 Samuel (Appendix S1A2; VII, chap. 9)
———. 2 Samuel (Appendix S1A2)
———. Matthew (V, chap. 9; VI, chap. 23; VII, chap. 9)
———. Luke (VI, chap. 19)
———. John (VII, chap. 13)
Borski, Robert. *The Long and the Short of It.* 2006. (Appendix S3A3)
Burroughs, Edgar Rice. *A Princess of Mars.* 1912. (VI, chap. 14)
———. *At the Earth's Core.* 1914. (VI, chap. 8)
———. *Chessmen of Mars.* 1922. (VI, chap. 14)
Burton, Francis. Translation of *The Book of the Thousand Nights and a Night.* 1885. (V, chap. 6; chap. 13)
Campbell, Joseph. "Spanish Lady" Irish folk song. (V, chap. 16)
Carroll, Lewis. "The Hunting of the Snark." 1876. (Appendix S3A5)
Cummings, Ray. *A Brand New World.* 1928. (Appendix SSA3)
De Camp, L. Sprague. Planet Krishna series. (V, chap. 12)
De Santillana, Giorgio and Hertha von Dechend, *Hamlet's Mill.* 1977. (VII, chap. 16)
Gordon, Joan. *Gene Wolfe.* 1986. (Appendix S3A5)
Hammett, Dashiell. *Red Harvest.* 1928. (VII, chap. 1; Appendix S2A2)

Herodotus. *The Histories.* Circa 430 BC. (V, chap. 12)
Homer. *The Odyssey.* (V, chap. 5; chap. 10; VII, chap. 12)
Hugo, Victor. *Les Misérables.* 1862. (VII, chap. 12)
Ives, Burl. "Dublin City" Irish folk song. (V, chap. 16)
Kurosawa, Akira. *Yojimbo.* 1961. (VI, chap. 1)
Lindsay, David. A Voyage to Arcturus. (Appendix S3A5)
London, Jack. "The Strength of the Strong." 1911. (V, Preface)
Plato's Cave. (V, chap. 2; VI, chap. 19; VII, chap. 20)
Pope, Alexander. Translation of Homer's *Odyssey.* 1828.
Prestor John. (V, chap. 2)
Sappho. Fragment of a poem: "As on the hills the shepherds trample the hyacinth under foot, and the flower darkens on the ground." (VII, Afterword)
"Sleeping Beauty." (VII, Preface)
Waterhouse, John William. *Diogenes.* 1882. (VI, chap. 2)
Wolfe, Gene. *Gene Wolfe's Orbital Thoughts.* 1992. (II, Dedication; V, chap. 2)

BOOKS BY THIS AUTHOR

Gene Wolfe's Book Of The New Sun: A Chapter Guide

A chapter-by-chapter guide to Gene Wolfe's "The Book of the New Sun," its sequel "The Urth of the New Sun," and four shorter works. Available in paperback, Kindle, and hardcover."crow,"

Roadside Picnic Revisited: Seven Articles On The Soviet Novel That Inspired The Film "Stalker"

A collection of essays and a book review relating to "Roadside Picnic," the Soviet science fiction novel by Arkady and Boris Strugatsky.

The Jizmatic Trilogy

A Pharmacist Visits Mars! Set your "fazer" to "freakout" in this mind-bending mashup of "John Carter" and "Naked Lunch." These are adventure tales in the style of circa 1912, but with strange currents of later eras.

www.ingramcontent.com/pod-product-compliance
Lightning Source LLC
Chambersburg PA
CBHW022112040426
42450CB00006B/674